BATTLE OF MANILA

NADIR OF JAPANESE BARBARISM, 3 FEBRUARY–3 MARCH 1945

MIGUEL MIRANDA

Pen & Sword
MILITARY

First published in Great Britain in 2019 by
PEN AND SWORD MILITARY
an imprint of
Pen and Sword Books Ltd
47 Church Street
Barnsley
South Yorkshire S70 2AS

ISBN 978 1 52672 905 7

Maps by George Anderson
In-text images where applicable are individually credited. Plate-section images are courtesy
Presidential Museum and Library PH, with relevant authorship credited accordingly
Typeset by Aura Technology and Software Services, India
Printed and bound by CPI Group (UK) Ltd., Croydon CR04YY

Pen & Sword Books Ltd incorporates the imprints of Pen & Sword
Archaeology, Atlas, Aviation, Battleground, Discovery, Family History, History, Maritime, Military,
Naval, Politics, Railways, Select, Social History, Transport, True Crime, Claymore Press, Frontline
Books, Leo Cooper, Praetorian Press, Remember When, Seaforth Publishing and Wharncliffe.

For a complete list of Pen and Sword titles please contact
Pen and Sword Books Limited
47 Church Street, Barnsley, South Yorkshire, S70 2AS, England
email: enquiries@pen-and-sword.co.uk
website: www.pen-and-sword.co.uk

Miguel Miranda, formerly a regional reporter, is an author from the Philippines and writes for several Pen & Sword military history series including 'Cold War 1945–1991' and 'History of Terror'. Writing about the battle of Manila has been an opportunity for him to confront a very dark period in Philippine history, one that is still misunderstood today. To amass the wealth of research and insight for this work he pored over volumes of official histories and archives, assembling a detailed narrative on the topic. Not only did the battle of Manila liberate the Philippines from cruel foreign domination but it set the stage for total independence in 1946. It bookended the American colonial period (1899–1945) and closed a chapter in a long saga of conflict and struggle that has visited his homeland again and again. As a country whose history is shaped by the designs of various empires, the battle of Manila showed how vital the Philippines is to the region, the gateway to the Asian landmass and the rampart of grand strategy for a would-be superpower. As it was then, as it is today.

CONTENTS

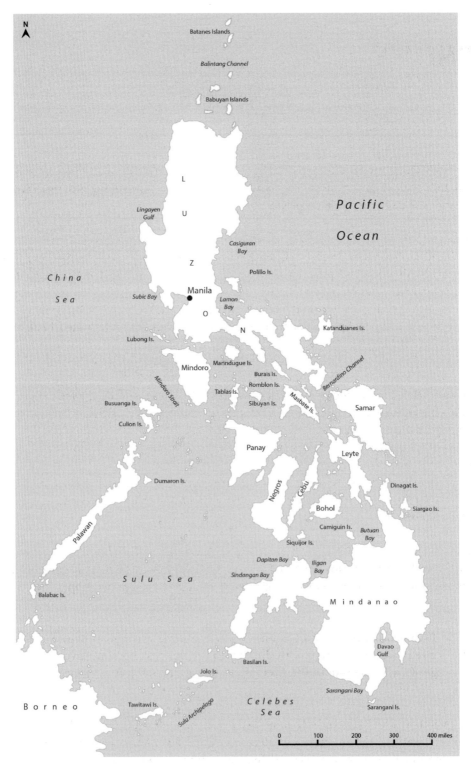

The Philippines.

TIMELINE

1896

August: Filipino revolutionaries in Cavite and Manila launch an uprising to overthrow Spain's colonial government. The local rebellion spreads to outlying provinces and a genuine war of independence begins

1898

March: A mysterious explosion sinks the USS *Maine* in Havana's harbour. The resulting outcry by the American press leads to the Spanish-American War. The lopsided battle of Manila Bay takes place two months later.

December: Tense negotiations in the French capital result in the Treaty of Paris where the US government pays $20 million for the rights to own Cuba, the Philippine Islands and Puerto Rico.

1899

February: Hostilities ensue in San Juan between the US Army in Luzon and the forces of the First Philippine Republic seeking to unify the country. This marks the beginning of Philippine-American War.

1902

July: US President Teddy Roosevelt announces the end of the Philippine-American War a year after General Emilio Aguinaldo is captured. Fighting continues in remote parts of the archipelago.

1917

April: The US formally joins the Allied Powers in World War I. The colonial government in the Philippines offers to raise a regiment of volunteers to fight in Europe.

1934

March: The impact of the Great Depression on the American economy revives the chance for a negotiated decoupling with the Philippine Islands. Filipino envoys hail the passage of the Tydings-McDuffie Act that sets a date for quasi-independence.

1935

15 November: The Philippine Commonwealth is inaugurated with a self-governing administration in place. President Manuel L. Quezon is its first head of state and all matters of national concern except defence are within his purview.

1937

August: Clashes in Peking between Chinese sentries and the Kwantung Army lead to the outbreak of the Second Sino-Japanese War. With militarists now leading the Japanese government, a full-scale invasion of China ensues.

1939

September: A Japanese attempt to penetrate the Mongolian steppe launches a short border war with the Soviet Union. A decisive clash in Kalkin Gol, or Nomonhan to the Japanese, leaves the Kwantung Army defeated. World War II begins in Europe when Germany and the Soviet Union invade Poland. In Asia, the Imperial Japanese Army's onslaught on China has bogged down.

1941

July: With the threat of a global war looming over Asia, the Philippine Commonwealth scrambles to raise a modern army. The retired MacArthur is made a 'field marshal' to command the fledgling Philippine military.

7 December: Waves of Japanese aircraft attack US Navy's warships in Pearl Harbor, Hawaii. A total of 21 ships are sunk and more than 2,000 Americans are killed. The invasion of the Philippines commences the following day.

24 December: As General Masaharu Homma's Fourteenth Army arrives in Central Luzon, MacArthur relocates his command to Corregidor Island. Manila is declared an open city to spare it from destruction.

1942

9 April: After three months of siege and deprivation, the thousands of American and Filipino soldiers trapped in the Bataan peninsula surrender to the Japanese. Several hundred Americans die as a result of their captors' brutality and maltreatment.

7 May: As Japanese troops pour into the beaches of Corregidor, General Jonathan Wainwright surrenders the garrison and marches into captivity. The Philippines is now fully under Japan's control.

1943

4 June: A Japanese armada is destroyed during an attempted invasion of Midway atoll. The material losses are so severe the entire course of the war in the Pacific begins to shift in the US's favour.

1944

1 August: Reduced to a leader-in-exile, President Manuel Quezon's faltering health leaves him bedridden for much of the year. He dies at Saranac Lake, New York, and is buried with full honours in Arlington Cemetery.

July: President Franklin D. Roosevelt makes a secret trip to Pearl Harbor to convene with the commanders of the Pacific theatre, including MacArthur. Rather than discuss an invasion of Formosa (Taiwan), MacArthur's insistence on liberating the Philippines prevails.

October: General Tomoyuki Yamashita arrives in the Philippines to command the Japanese Army's defence of the islands. Like MacArthur in 1941, Yamashita is doomed to witness his carefully laid plans crumble.

19 October: An American armada carrying X and XIV Corps arrives in Leyte Gulf. The largest naval battle in history ensues and the liberation of the Philippines commences.

1945

9 January: XIV Corps is delivered to an undefended Lingayen Gulf. Rather than meet stiff resistance, Japanese defences in Central Luzon are sporadic and scattered. On 29 January XI Corps lands at Subic Bay.

31 January: General Robert Eichelberger's 11th Airborne is brought to Nasugbu in Southern Luzon. Their objective is to capture the surrounding hills, flush them of Japanese holdouts, and proceed to Manila.

3 February: Troops and tanks belonging to the 44th Battalion, 8th Cavalry Regiment storm the University of Santo Tomas, which is used as a prison for American civilians. Rather than fight, the small Japanese detachment agrees to surrender. The battle for Manila commences.

7 February: 11th Airborne attacks the heavily defended Genko Line that cuts across Parañaque. Despite the lack of artillery and tank support, the paratroopers manage to overwhelm the Japanese.

12 February: Manila is completely encircled by the 37th Infantry Division and the 7th Cavalry Division. Thousands of Japanese naval infantry remain holed up in buildings and houses, ready to fight till the end.

17 February: With the last Japanese holdouts still in control of Intramuros, a multi-pronged assault is launched to eliminate them. The walls of the old city are blasted with howitzers and tanks and troops clear the buildings inside.

22–23 February: One of the most complex operations in the Luzon campaign gets underway. The 6th Ranger Battalion liberates the internment camp in Los Baños where hundreds of American PoWs are held.

23 February: Intramuros and its nearby administrative buildings are finally cleared after several days of gruelling combat. But there's little to celebrate. Entire neighbourhoods are destroyed and homeless residents are left to fend for themselves.

2 September: As Japanese forces in Luzon are now all but annihilated, the Pacific theatre winds down. Japan formally surrenders to the Allies in a grim ceremony aboard the battleship USS *Missouri* in Tokyo Bay.

1946

4 July: With Manila and other cities still in ruins, the Philippines gains full independence from the United States as agreed upon during the inception of the Commonwealth. President Manuel Roxas is the republic's first head of state.

INTRODUCTION

What happens when a particular country devotes all its energies to global conquest? In the case of Japan, it led to a gradual yet violent expansion lasting from 1894 until 1942 that culminated in two atomic bombs dropped on its cities; the Allies' final victory in 1945 meant Japan's quest for empire never paid off. But Japan came so very close to achieving its goals during the struggle its own history books call the Great Pacific War or sometimes the Greater East Asia War rather than World War II. What undid the infernal designs of Tokyo's militarists was a robust American economy that outfought and overwhelmed the tenuous Co-Prosperity Sphere that briefly existed when Japanese force of arms had evicted western militaries from Southeast Asia.

It can still be argued how Japan's short-lived dominion over Manchuria or its occupation of Formosa were more reasonable goals for its martial empire. Yet it is beyond any doubt the road to total defeat had its last stretch in the Philippines. It was in October 1944 when a decisive sea battle in Leyte decided the fate of the Imperial Japanese Navy (IJN) and the losses suffered from an unstoppable American invasion so crippled the Japanese military that it never again managed to launch a genuine offensive campaign anywhere.

But the months of arduous combat it took for the Allies to liberate the Philippines did have a terrible consequence and this is the subject of the present volume. What follows is a blow-by-blow account of Japan's sudden conquest of the Philippine Commonwealth, which, at the time, caused the worst defeat in US military history, and the monumental effort to free the country that climaxed with an unnecessary battle for Manila. This should be the vital lesson learned from the tragedy that unfolded over February and March 1945. When intelligence and logistics fail in the course of modern war, horrific outcomes should be expected. It is ironic how the US Army divisions tasked with seizing Manila, like the token Japanese garrison that remained, did not expect to fight over the city. The 37th Infantry Division was anticipating jubilant crowds in the neighbourhoods abandoned by the retreating Japanese and there were plans for a victory march across the Luneta in impeccable columns. Meanwhile, the Manila Naval Defence Force under Admiral Iwabuchi Sanji did intend to withdraw and escape from the Americans but poor timing and the total breakdown of the Japanese command structure in Luzon meant 16,000 Japanese holdouts decided to go down fighting instead: their final orders never arrived. When the last pockmarked government buildings in Manila had been cleared barely a hundred Japanese prisoners were left to collect.

The battle for Manila didn't have to take place, but it did and a whole city was razed in the span of three weeks. Since its population weren't allowed to flee or seek shelter elsewhere, the fighting left a civilian death toll, the exact figures of which remain uncertain until now. This is another bitter irony of the battle—General Douglas MacArthur

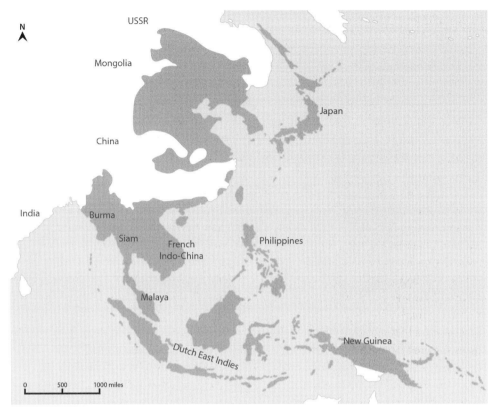

The Japanese Co-Prosperity Sphere.

himself forbade the Army Air Forces from conducting bombing runs anywhere over Manila to avoid collateral damage. On the ground, however, the 37th Infantry and 1st Cavalry Division had little choice but to use artillery to take out Japanese fortifications at close range.

The Americans did value Manila and its citizens. Thousands of servicemen and their families had lived in the city before the war. MacArthur himself, who was entrusted to build a national army for the Philippine Commonwealth, lived in a sumptuous penthouse in the iconic Manila Hotel that had a splendid view of the sea. It was also rumoured he had a mistress ensconced at a different address outside the city.

But what value did Manila have for the Japanese occupation? Of course, when their tanks and troops marched on the 'Open City' in January 1942 the city was abandoned by its defenders to spare its inhabitants from a cruel siege. Yet in January 1941 Iwabuchi's men toiled for days putting up road blocks and pillboxes to frustrate the American advance.

To understand the importance of Manila, a broader context for Japan's actions in World War II is needed. The United States only fought its greatest Asian adversary for three years and seven months, a period spanning Pearl Harbor to V-J Day. Japan, on the

Admiral Thomas
C. Hart, Philippine
president Manuel
Quezon and future
US-congresswoman
Clare Boothe Luce,
October 1941. (Library
of Congress)

other hand, had been prosecuting a ground war in Asia from 1937, when it launched a unilateral invasion of China from Manchuria, until it expanded its war effort to a full-scale invasion of Southeast Asia, followed by total defeat a few years later.

Making sense of Japan's actions during this period means going back to the Tokugawa Shogunate's ebb in the mid-19th century. Beginning with Commodore Perry's forceful naval expedition in 1853 to open trade between Japan and the United States, a gradual revolution occurred in Japan's political life that transformed the country. The abolition of the Shogunate and the Samurai class that defined the Meiji Restoration, followed by a detailed programme for industrializing while the authority of autonomous feudal lords was greatly diminished, allowed for a centralized state bureaucracy to emerge. By 1889 Japan's new imperial system, which enshrined the Emperor as a lifelong ruler and figurehead above a functioning parliament led by an elected chief executive, adopted the

This photo says everything about the US influence in the Philippines. Here American businessman C. A. Dewitt meets President Manuel Quezon, probably around 1940. (George Grantham Bain Collection, Library of Congress)

Prussian constitution and began to import as much Western technology it could afford. This resulted in a new, modern Japan, an ancient country that had grafted the salient features of the most powerful European states unto its governance model.

It isn't surprising how Japan quickly embraced aggressive expansionism to secure additional territory and resources. This began with the Sino-Japanese War of 1894/5 that allowed it to wrest the island of Formosa and the Korean peninsula from the ailing Qing Dynasty that ruled over China. A broad rearmament took place in the intervening years leading to the Russo-Japanese War of 1904/5 that ended with a humiliating defeat for Tsar Nicholas's bumbling navy at Tsushima. World War I and the Russian Civil War allowed the Imperial Japanese Army and Navy to rehearse small-scale expeditionary campaigns beyond East Asia.

During the 1910s and 1920s Tokyo pursued a vast colonial project to build infrastructure connecting the Korean Peninsula with Manchuria. This meant raw materials from the latter territory could be processed in factories established with Japanese expertise and financing in the former territory. A proto-state soon emerged called Manchukuo that served as an agricultural–industrial hub governed by a sizeable garrison. As the global economy subsided in the 1930s as a result of the Great Depression, militarist factions in Japan's armed forces began to agitate for an ultra-nationalist foreign policy. Their platform was a strange mix of xenophobia and manifest destiny and represented a unique model for attaining regional dominance that no other Asian country has ever copied. The unchecked rise of Japanese militarism culminated in the 1936 putsch where militarists strong-armed the Diet—Japan's parliament—to set the nation on a warpath. The same militarists used their newfound clout to crush any form of dissent, whether through assassination or imprisonment. That same year marked the beginning of the Second Sino-Japanese War as Japanese troops overran Peiping (Beijing) and Shanghai. The Chinese capital, Nanking, fell in 1937 and its inhabitants bore the brunt of the Japanese army's atrocities.

As Japan committed its industries to producing war matériel and kept annexing more territory, the United States imposed punitive sanctions in July 1941 when Tokyo declared French Indochina a 'protectorate' soon after Paris surrendered to the Nazis. For Japan's unrepentant militarists, cutting off imports of oil and precious metals was the last outrage from Washington DC. To achieve its aim of conquering Asia and establishing a regional bloc it could govern, elaborate plans were drawn to neutralize the American, British, French and Dutch navies whose ships guarded the vital sea lanes that sustained the homeland.

Invading the Philippines became an important objective for two reasons. First, it had the largest concentration of American forces in Asia. Second, it would provide the IJN new facilities and ports for protecting their Southeast Asian dominion. Remarkably, the intelligence by the Imperial Army and Navy on conditions in the Philippines were superb—flights of spy planes were never detected—and there were few problems assessing the strength of the archipelago's defences; a combination of shoddy planning and carelessness on the part of the US military in the Philippines meant the Imperial Navy's air fleets knew precisely where to strike and when. The final war plan for the Philippines involved a combined air and amphibious assault on the island of Luzon, the main objective being the capital Manila, and the southernmost island of Mindanao. These two thrusts would be like a set of massive jaws devouring the Philippines.

Japan did prevail in its quest for hegemony. The Philippines was defeated in less than six months, with the final holdouts surrendering in May 1942. What followed next were three years of deprivation and occupation as a martial law regime was established across the country. But with liberation imminent in early 1945, one last cruel battle needed to be fought. Three American divisions—the 37th Infantry and 1st Cavalry bearing down from the north, and the 11th Airborne pushing from the south—were tasked with retaking the a city once romanticized as the 'Pearl of the Orient'. What follows is an account of their struggle to free Manila.

1. MACARTHUR'S BITTER DEFEAT

Barely a day after the surprise attack on Pearl Harbor, formations of Japanese aircraft entered Luzon's airspace and struck every conceivable military target on the ground. The idle rows of B-17 bombers at Clark Field in Pampanga were destroyed with ease and the few American P-40Bs that managed to launch were unable to thwart the waves of twin-engine Mitsubishi Bettys and the escorting Zeroes coming from Formosa. In the span of two days Japan had imposed near complete air superiority over the Philippines. It was an unprecedented disaster for the United States Armed Forces in the Far East (USAFFE) whose precious few months of preparation went to naught and doomed the Philippine Commonwealth, a semi-independent statehood granted to the Philippines as a former American colony. Full independence was years away, scheduled for 4 July 1946.

Manuel L. Quezon, the Philippine Commonwealth's first head of state.

Even the Commonwealth's first head of state, President Manuel L. Quezon, stood helpless as Japanese bombers pulverized Baguio, the scenic 'summer capital' cradled in the Cordillera mountains of Northern Luzon. The president was holidaying with his eldest daughter at an official residence when General Douglas MacArthur rang him. The ageing commander of all military forces in the Commonwealth had just been told by his own staff of events in distant Pearl Harbor when they caught the news on the radio. To Quezon's dismay, MacArthur was the one to inform him that a state of war now existed between America and Japan. Then the sound of distant engines compelled Quezon to walk outside the living room and look skyward. He watched in horror as bombs fell on the defenceless city below.

The past year had been a frantic one. Since the founding of the Philippine Commonwealth in 1935, plans were drawn up to raise a national army of 400,000 men. Quezon's longstanding friendship with MacArthur, who was within rights to enjoy his retirement, brought the decorated commander back into uniform as a 'field marshal' to oversee the entire programme. The resulting plan was laughable in hindsight, an imaginative pursuit rather than tangible policy. MacArthur looked to imitate the Swiss conscription system where a small professional force was cultivated to take charge of a vast reservist army. He also envisioned a pocket navy of torpedo boats and an air fleet no other Asian country could afford. At the very least, these far-fetched plans led to the construction of the Philippine Military Academy outside Baguio, an institution patterned after MacArthur's own beloved alma mater. But implementing the Philippine National Defence Act passed by Quezon's legislature seemed too ambitious. By 1941, none of its lofty goals had come to fruition and Washington had little choice but mobilize the USAFFE and reinstate General MacArthur as its supreme commander. Perhaps there was no better qualified individual for the task. No American past or present has influenced the course of a foreign country's history the way MacArthur impacted the Philippines. His own father was a Civil War veteran and a distinguished general in the Philippine-American War, leading the volunteer regiments that subdued the faraway Spanish colony as his son finished his studies at West Point, where he graduated with honors. As a junior officer, the young MacArthur was a foreign observer allowed to embed with the Japanese in their short yet bloody conflict with Russia over Port Arthur in 1904. He was recommended the Congressional Medal of Honor on two occasions for his sterling leadership and after World War I rose to become the US Army's Chief of Staff.

His last known mission in service of the United States government was deploying cavalrymen to Washington DC to put down the Bonus Army picketing the government. On that fateful summer in 1932 thousands of impoverished veterans, once eager doughboys sent to beat the Kaiser in the last world conflict, were agitating for a much-deserved payout from the federal government. MacArthur led a cavalry formation supported by tanks and charged the Bonus Army with sabres, the flat side of the blades working as splendid pacifying tools. But what truly set MacArthur apart was his lifestyle away from home. His personal residence in the Philippines was a well-appointed penthouse at the Manila Hotel offering an unspoiled view of tree-lined Dewey Boulevard. In 1938 he

Filipino casualties on the first day of Philippine-American War, Santa Ana, 5 February 1899. (NARA / US ARC Identifier: 524389)

married an American expatriate, Jean Marie Faircloth, who bore him a son whose entire childhood would encompass the two great conflicts that involved his father, World War II and the Korean War. A highly regarded public figure and quasi-celebrity in Manila during the 1930s, MacArthur's personal connections to the local elite—matched with a voluminous knowledge of the archipelago's geography—made him the ideal candidate for helping the Commonwealth get on its feet in uncertain times.

Under MacArthur's command in 1941 were a total of 22,532 American servicemen, including the elite Philippine Scouts, augmented by the Philippine Constabulary—a colonial gendarmerie led by US Army officers—and an untrained and untested multitude of Filipinos hurriedly recruited throughout the archipelago. Thanks to the US War Department's newfound sense of urgency, hurried shipments of arms and equipment brought almost 200 aircraft, at least two tank battalions, and additional batteries of 75mm and 105mm howitzers to the Philippines. These shipments added to the arsenal MacArthur had at his disposal in the Philippines. M1917 Enfield rifles left over from 1918 were still piled up in warehouses and became standard issue for the USAFFE. There were enormous bases scattered throughout Luzon, including the Clark aerodrome at Pampanga—at least two hours' drive north of Manila—and the immaculate Camp John Hay at Baguio. The most formidable was the island fortress of Corregidor with its gigantic batteries protecting the entrance to Manila Bay. The capital itself was ringed with defences. The supply depots in nearby Cavite and Bataan were guarded by rings of anti-aircraft guns. A functioning aerodrome in Nichols Field near Fort McKinley allowed interceptors to protect Manila. There were no viable passages for enemy forces to attack the city from the sea or any other direction, unless they came down from the north across the plains of Central Luzon.

So confident was MacArthur of the forces at his disposal he even approved the Far East Air Force's commissioning on 3 November with General Lewis H. Brereton leading it. On paper, MacArthur's entire command looked formidable, stacked with elderly veterans with impeccable reputations. The elaborate defences on the main island of Luzon were to be directed by General Jonathan M. Wainwright as commander of the North Luzon Force that had four infantry divisions. A separate South Luzon Force was meant to guard against any amphibious landings. Meanwhile, the islands of the Visayas ('the island of Negros') and the entirety of Mindanao had token commands assigned to them. Supplies of food and fuel were abundant and American forces lived comfortably. Their Filipino counterparts? Not quite so much. A regular army hadn't existed in the Philippines since

Lieutenant General Masaharu Homma arrives in the Philippines at the head of the Fourteenth Army.

it became an American colony after its conquest of 1899–1902. The thousands of boys—plucked from their schools and villages—who enthusiastically flocked to enlist had no inkling of military life. With the exception of the Philippine Scouts, who were at the very least adept cavalrymen, the local divisions that were swelled with Filipino recruits had neither the time nor the resources to assume a cohesive form and function well under a chain of command.

It was the story state of the Filipino conscripts that further eroded the USAFFE's carefully prepared plans for holding the Commonwealth until reinforcements arrived from Australia and Hawaii, which they never did. After the crippling airstrikes in the first and second weeks of December, Japanese troops were spotted in separate landings around Luzon—aside from the prosperous town of Vigan, these missions targeted remote areas—and Mindanao. A detachment even entered Davao, a coastal city in Mindanao known for having a large Japanese diaspora, without coming up against serious resistance. On 22 December a Japanese fleet arrived in Lingayen Gulf, an unprotected bay 150 kilometres north of Manila, and discharged 43,000 troops of the Fourteenth Army led by Lieutenant General Masaharu Homma. Educated in the West and a fluent English-speaker, Homma's credentials appeared tailor-made for knocking the Americans out of their largest overseas territory. The invasion force under his command had mustered in Formosa and sailed undetected until they reached Philippine waters, but a sole report by a loitering US Navy submarine failed to alert USAFFE HQ of their presence. At the onset of the invasion, Homma's anxiety over a possible counterattack meant he couldn't be bothered to join his troops at the beach until the majority of them disembarked. Most of the Japanese soldiers under his command, in fact, weren't told their destination until the last minute. The importance of the operation, however, weighed heaviest on their commander. From 22 December onward he had just 50 days to conquer the entire Philippines and vanquish the Americans. His worries extended beyond the beach at Lingayen as a rapid march over Central Luzon risked exposing the Fourteenth Army's flank to any attack from the Cordillera mountain range whose peaks offered superb vantage points for observing the progress of the Japanese divisions.

A mere 24 hours after the Fourteenth Army arrived in Lingayen, a bitterly disappointed MacArthur told Quezon he might need to evacuate with his family to Corregidor, where a complex of underground tunnels could support thousands. The nerve-wracked Quezon, almost bedridden from heartache and the onset of tuberculosis, acquiesced. The announcement of Manila's status as an 'open city' was a minor consolation for the Commonwealth government as a siege would have invited carpet bombing and the unwanted miseries of privation and scarcity. (Manila's residents were already learning to cope with the latter, as shops had imposed rationing the day the war started.) The fearsome presence of Japanese bombers was an unpleasant reminder for Manila's population. Visions of Guernica, Shanghai, Warsaw, Leningrad, and London under relentless aerial bombardment were enough to humble even the most ardent patriot. Proclaiming an 'open city' meant there would be no defiant last stand in Manila. USAFFE HQ revised its current plans and initiated the WPO-1 contingency drawn up by US Army tacticians

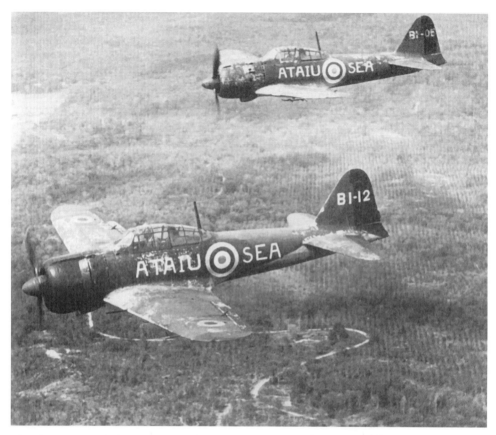

Mitsubishi Zeroes were the best dog-fighters in the Pacific at the beginning of the war—but not at the end. Pictured are two captured samples being flown in 1945 by Allied pilots.

before the Commonwealth was established. The so-called War Plan Orange required all American troops and their auxiliaries to evacuate the capital and fortify the mountainous Bataan peninsula that formed the upper half of Manila Bay. Its forested terrain blocked any passage from Central Luzon and its beaches offered a splendid view of the South China Sea. Corregidor was close by too, with its multiple batteries able to repel any approaching warships. But none ever came. With their air superiority unchallenged, the Japanese besieged the island with waves of bombers.

Although Homma's Fourteenth Army smashed across the lines of defence arranged by Wainwright in Central Luzon, their progress was marred too. Superb army and naval aviation—Japan's military didn't have an air force *per se*—succeeded at scattering the USAFFE's logistics but the pressure of moving at a rapid clip to reach Manila was hard on the Fourteenth Army's men. The Japanese learned to fear the M3 Stuart tanks and the self-propelled mounts or SPMs whose armor was thick enough to withstand machine-gun bullets. The latter were half-tracks carrying 75mm howitzers that served as mobile artillery. Another rude surprise was the M1917 Browning machine gun that spat .30-calibre bullets at such a high velocity it could cut a Japanese soldier in half. The M1917 performed so well in the Philippines it went on to serve the rest of the war in the hands of marines, sailors, soldiers and militia alike, always a dependable terror for the enemy. The Philippine Scouts put up a gallant resistance on horseback, picking off enemy Japanese with their .45 pistols. To slow the Fourteenth Army's progress, rail crossings and bridges were fortified if they couldn't be demolished timeously. But to the disappointment of the Americans, the Filipinos made a poor effort in holding back the enemy. Some USAFFE veterans who recounted their war in the Philippines didn't mince words when it came to reminiscences of the Filipino's reluctant soldiering: the enmity toward the Japanese may have smoldered in their psyche but this didn't always translate into valorous conduct in the thick of the action.

Tokyo's war plans had the same consideration as Washington DC's: reinforcements from Hawaii and elsewhere would be steaming toward the archipelago as soon as a ground invasion began. Indeed, before the year was out the cruiser USS *Pensacola* was leading a convoy to relieve the embattled USAFFE, whose broadcasts in the Commonwealth kept reassuring the civilian population of coming relief. Unfortunately, the convoy was diverted to Australia where the War Department sought to open a new front for rolling back Japan's aggression. No relief was coming to the Philippines.

Homma's exhausted troops reached Manila after Christmas Day and rather than exult in their latest victory, the Fourteenth Army wasted an entire week trying to reorganize its logistics. The Imperial Japanese Army in 1941 was unequalled throughout Asia, but it was neither equipped nor supplied to the same standard as the American or British armies. This brief lapse bought time for Wainwright to gather his men inside Bataan, whose towering peaks formed natural barriers against direct attack. For the civilians in Manila abandoned by the USAFFE however, the arrival of their new occupiers was nothing to celebrate. The Americans had been conquerors of the Philippines less than half a century prior and the regime they imposed saw a radical transformation in local culture and habits. American rule might have got off to a bitter start, with a pitiless counterinsurgency and heavy-handed governance reminiscent of the worst European imperialism, but American colonial governance led to public education and colleges, a civil service and a quasi-democracy, nice cars and the irresistible lure of the silver screen. Since the turn of the century American culture poured into the Philippines without restraint, planting jazz, lounge singers and ritzy nightclubs in the public consciousness. Now that the Japanese were in charge, would they do the same as the Americanos and refashion the Filipinos in their own image?

New Year's Eve in 1941 was a hopeful affair. The USAFFE command celebrated in the tunnels of Corregidor, where ample stocks of liquor and processed meat were a rare distraction for the thousands trapped in the island. The Quezons and MacArthurs bonded too, with the USAFFE commander's four-year-old son Arthur treated like a nephew by the withered president of the Commonwealth. Meanwhile, in Bataan, American and Filipino troops gorged on their rations and whatever niceties could be scrounged.

Filipino soldiers had no problems finding rice and knew how to forage for chickens and pigs while Americans were reliant on a diminishing supply of canned food. This was a strange contrast that made life harder for USAFFE personnel as the months wore on. Decades of colonization hadn't acclimatized American palettes to the local cuisine and an unforeseen weakness in the USAFFE's plans was the burden of maintaining adequate stocks of preserved food. Such a liability hasn't been emphasized enough in chronicles of the war in the Pacific. American stomachs found it difficult adjusting to a suitable diet in the tropics and the disease and sickness that afflicted GIs left an unmistakable toll.

Fighting resumed in the first week of January 1942 as constant air raids over Bataan eroded morale and increased the gnawing desperation among the men condemned to hold as long as possible. Two months into the war and USAFFE HQ was still fanning hopes of reinforcements arriving by sea. MacArthur himself reassured a doubtful Quezon of imminent victory. "I will bring you in triumph on the points of my bayonets to Manila," he told the beleaguered president.

But what kept USAFFE fighting week after week was the impressive organization it maintained under the greatest strain. The Bataan Peninsula was halved between two armies, I and II Philippine Corps, with nearly a 100,000 troops between them. The corps were divided into three parallel sectors, two lines of resistance manned by whole divisions and a base area at the rear for the local command posts and logistics sent from Corregidor. There was no further friendly air cover to shield Bataan from the Japanese navy's bombers but enough machine guns and artillery were available to hold off repeated assaults. This didn't stop the Japanese Fourteenth Army from attempting to overrun Bataan in a costly amphibious assault in late January, where two regiments were landed along the peninsula's southwestern beaches. Another pause followed, as Homma grew dispirited by mounting casualties. His available manpower was simply not enough for securing the entirety of the Philippines and the strict timetable set by Tokyo soon elapsed. Fresh divisions arrived from Hong Kong and China in February and Homma readied his plans for a last major offensive to smash the USAFFE in Bataan.

Unknown to the Japanese, MacArthur had already arranged for his escape from the Philippines on 12 March, taking his family and staff with him and leaving Wainwright in charge. This exit made sense considering the fate of Singapore a few months later. It was better for America's highest-ranking soldier in Asia to leave a doomed mission for the sake of leading his forces in a fresh campaign. But if MacArthur's odyssey under cover of darkness seemed an unspoken admission that he failed, it seems to appear dastardly in light of Quezon's parting gift. In the spirit of utmost friendship and just recompense for services rendered, MacArthur did receive a monetary handout worth $500,000 from the Philippine treasury. Perhaps it was better for Quezon's beloved 'Field Marshal' to receive the sum: if the money was left behind it would have been rendered useless or likely stolen. In late April a US Navy minelayer unloaded silver bullion from the Philippine Treasury into the waters off Corregidor hoping to spare it from plunder. The reasoning went that as long as the Japanese never found the hoard it could be pulled from the depths after the war to help with reconstruction. MacArthur and his entourage

This iconic photo from early 1942 captures the triumph of Japanese arms in Luzon.

travelled by boat for a day and a night until they reached the Mindanao coast and went by car to the airstrip at the Del Monte fruit company's plantation. (The Commonwealth had a thriving economy fed by agricultural exports, which was another crucial aspect of America's dominion over the Philippines.) Taken by plane to Australia, MacArthur assumed command of the Southwest Pacific Area (SWPA) and laid down a strategy for chipping away at Japan's hard-won empire. It seemed miraculous how he avoided the shameful responsibility of leading the USAFFE—soon renamed the United States Army in the Philippines or USAPHIL—to total defeat. He left behind officers and soldiers who had nothing except doubt and forlorn hope about their circumstances. Always savvy with handling the press, MacArthur framed his getaway from the Philippines as an expedient setback. He delivered the timeless vow of a promised return at some point in the future to save the Filipino people from Japan's barbarity. An earlier act of self-preservation was Quezon's own journey to permanent exile on 18 February. Because of his poor health and value as the Commonwealth's first elected leader, Quezon's reluctant departure needed a more elaborate setup. The submarine USS *Swordfish* awaited its high-profile guests, penetrating the naval blockade in Corregidor on its way to the Visayas. After a month in hiding, the Quezons travelled to Mindano and from there flew to Australia on 26 March, finally reaching American soil in late April.

The final offensive to crush the resistance at Bataan started on 3 April with an artillery barrage that set the dry *cogon* grass on fire around the perimeter held by the main line of resistance. The Filipino divisions wilted, their hapless troops cowering in foxholes and trenches, until the wall of fiery death raised an unstoppable panic. In the span of a day, the gallant Filipinos who were celebrated in Allied propaganda as indomitable warriors battling stupendous odds fled to the American lines. There were no reinforcements arriving from Corregidor, whose tunnels now housed thousands of frightened Americans surviving day to day on strict rations. The situation in the peninsula was hopeless and with ammunition nearly depleted and no means of escape, the last orders from Wainwright's HQ sank American resolve: Corregidor expected an immediate counterattack to drive the Japanese back to Subic in the northwest. But before the week was out an exhausted General Edward P. King endured the humiliation that MacArthur had narrowly avoided. After an impromptu conference with a Japanese officer who barely spoke English, the USAPHIL force surrendered within 48 hours, leaving Corregidor the last feeble bastion held by the US military in Asia.

The phenomenon of total defeat against an exotic foe wasn't the only ordeal to burden the Americans in Bataan. With few contingencies for so many prisoners, Homma's commanders devised a straightforward plan. Without bothering to wait for adequate transport, American and Filipino troops were forced to walk a hundred kilometres on foot. Their destination was Camp O'Donnell, a temporary holding pen for detainees until better accommodations became available. Once the exodus began under pain of excruciating death—the Japanese soldiers always had their bayonets fixed—the month of April turned into the first well-known outrage committed by Japan's army in the Philippines. Wracked by dysentery and hunger, wounds festering and untreated, hundreds of Americans died from the ordeal. Even more Filipinos perished from the cruelty of the contemptuous Japanese, whose disdain for surrendered foes had left a bloody legacy in China. In the absence of accurate figures that haven't been tallied to this day, the infamous Bataan Death March claimed one out of four soldiers who took part. American GIs had never before put up with such shame and depravity. But it was the Filipinos who did most of the dying.

With the subjugation of Bataan only Corregidor was left. A combined Japanese air and sea assault was the fierce death blow that smothered the rocky island and compelled Wainwright to follow his conscience and spare the 10,000-odd civilians and soldiers left with him from a massacre. Stumbling out of the battered Malinta Tunnel on 8 May, one month after Bataan's abject surrender, a sorrowful Wainwright struggled to hold back tears as his people marched into captivity. The US military had never experienced defeat on the scale of the Philippines in 1942. Neither had any US command's highest-ranking officer, in this case MacArthur, ever abandoned an entire country to spare himself from suffering the consequence of his poor leadership. With the fall of the Philippines a victorious Japan reached its peak as the uncontested Great Power in the Asia-Pacific. But the United States was far from beaten.

President Quezon: dying in exile

With his genteel manners and unfailing tact, the first President of the Philippine Commonwealth can hardly be described as a warrior-statesman. But war and its miseries were the defining moments of Manuel Quezon's storied life. Born in a *barrio* idyll—a hamlet called Baler—and raised poor, by his early 20s the dashing Quezon was an untrained officer of the First Republic that met its match during the Philippine-American War of 1898–1905. Wracked by exhaustion and malaria, Quezon had the accidental privilege of an audience with General Arthur MacArthur when trying to ascertain whether or not the revolutionary leader General Emilio Aguinaldo was being kept prisoner in Malacañang Palace. Of course, it was MacArthur's son Douglas whom he would promote to the titular rank of Field Marshal in the same Malacañang Palace three decades later.

To succeed in the American colonial regime, Quezon taught himself English and passed the bar, thereby affording him a decent livelihood as an attorney. But he never forgot the trials he overcame in his youth; he once told an audience of college students, "You know I worked in the rice field, I waited at table, I did a lot of odd things. I passed nights without any food. So why can't others do what I myself did?"

But Quezon's oratorical talent and professional connections brought him to the forefront of national politics. Upon winning the presidency of the Commonwealth, Quezon had a few advantages over other post-colonial leaders: a vibrant capital city

Manuel Quezon during a visit to China, 1937.

filled with brilliant architecture, a loyal cabinet of administrators and an economy fuelled by agricultural exports. Of course, once war broke out in December 1941, Quezon fell ill from the stress and grief brought about by seeing the Philippines succumb once more to a foreign invader. Equally fluent in English, Spanish and Tagalog and trusted by the Americans, Quezon escaped from Corregidor with a heavy heart as the Philippine surrender became imminent. Weakened by his illness, Quezon died on 1 August 1944, at his residence at Saranac Lake and was given a temporary burial in Arlington Cemetery, Washington DC. His remains were sent home to the Philippines on 27 July 1946.

2. LEYTE TO LINGAYEN

The Allies momentarily defeated in Southeast Asia, the Philippines slid under Japanese control. Where once Americans and European expatriates enjoyed privileged lives running the local economy, the Japanese occupiers erased their presence overnight. For the thousands of soldiers who surrendered in Bataan and Corregidor and were herded inside internment camps a new nightmare began. American PoWs in particular were sent to Japan as slave labour, crammed inside ships for a hellish maritime transit. Upon arriving at port they were assigned to toil in mines and factories owned by the great corporations that furnished Tokyo's war machine.

In the newly occupied Philippines the Japanese sought out any foreigners, American or not, living in Manila. The old University of Santo Tomas, a relic from the Spanish colonial era, was turned into a concentration camp. Here was another ruthless exercise, less depraved than the recent Death March, where civilians of different ages were robbed of their liberty for the vaguest reasons. The purpose of converting the campus into a prison was never justified. Being a scholastic institution established in the 17th century as Spain's colonial regime consolidated its authority over the Philippines, the location was suspect. To imprison children with their parents and force a strict diet on the internees did little to improve the menacing reputation of the Japanese military government.

To placate the worst fears harbored by Filipinos of the fate of their nascent country, Lieutenant General Homma delivered a speech before the

Jouge B. Vargas, a secretary of President Manuel Luis Quezon's, meets General Homma Masaharu of the Imperial Japanese Army, February 1943.

remnants of the Commonwealth government that could be gathered in Manila. He was the first Asian military leader to have defeated an American army on equal terms, an historical achievement of some magnitude. Even if this fact was never acknowledged, for a brief period in 1942, Homma was the unchallenged overlord of the country. No wonder he sought to gently remind those gathered of Japan's unassailable position at the time. "You all know that within less than six months of the war, Japan already holds the supremacy of the Pacific," he said.

With unsettling bluntness, Homma's overtures to the Filipino public sought to erase the trauma of the past month's fighting. "Since landing in the Philippines ... I gave explicit orders to my men to treat the Filipino people with kindness and to refrain from endangering their daily existence." He also extended an olive branch, albeit wrapped in a hazy concept that had resonated with Japanese propagandists for the past decade, The Greater East Asia Co-Prosperity Sphere: "It is imperative that the Filipino people identify themselves with this great ideal. As a leopard cannot change its spots, you cannot alter the fact that you are Orientals. Why should you follow the dictates of Europe or America with an inferiority complex?"

So there it was. Homma had breathed life into a new order that celebrated the primacy of Asians over the cruel imperialism of the United States and Europe. But was Japan's imposition of its Co-Prosperity Sphere a genuine effort to deliver millions from colonial bondage or was it a blunt propaganda tactic to hide the fact that a militarist–industrial system now had free reign over a dozen conquered nations? Had those parts of China occupied by Japan for years rejoiced at their circumstances? Were not the Korean peninsula and Formosa outright colonies too?

Undaunted by exile, President Quezon was appalled by Japan's colonial designs on his country and the methods by which these were imposed. "The Filipino is, psychologically speaking, a Westerner," he reflected in his memoir. "Of all the excesses committed by the Japanese, those which insulted the dignity and honor of Filipinos are without doubt the ones that will leave the deepest and most irreconcilable wounds."

With Manila's expatriate population imprisoned as the Co-Prosperity Sphere was being rolled out, taking their place were hundreds of Japanese who, just like the Americans before them, were allowed to run businesses and provide essential services for the occupying regime. As if the parallels to American rule weren't striking enough, the Japanese wasted no time cobbling together a Filipino administration to govern on their behalf. As an incentive, the same US-educated *pensionados* who devoted themselves to the Commonwealth were given the choice of either joining the new puppet government or face a firing squad.

As the latest member of the Co-Prosperity Sphere the Philippine Commonwealth was even given a new identity as a 'Second Republic' whose independence was scheduled to take place in October 1943. Oddly, the very same US-educated managers and technocrats working for the Second Republic distrusted the Japanese regime and harboured unrepentant pro-American sensibilities. The so-called 'Puppet President' of the occupation years, Salvador 'Doy' Laurel, was a former Justice of the Supreme Court and like many

The slum-like dwellings inside the old University of Santo Tomas housed thousands of 'internees'. (LIFE / Presidential Museum and Library)

of his peers owed his accomplishments to the American educational system that produced a new class of Filipino civil servants with liberal-democratic sensibilities. There was an undeniable fondness for America but also an awareness that earnest nationalism, rather than supplication to a colonial power, was the way forward. The Commonwealth embodied this ideal best, not the Co-Prosperity Sphere established by force of arms. As President Laurel's administration commenced in 1943, there was no end to its shortcomings. Foremost was the reluctance of cabinet members and managers from the vanquished Quezon administration to resume work for fear of being branded as collaborators. Although some did assume positions of influence, they often did so with heavy hearts and no small amount of rationalization. As Japanese troops and their equipment

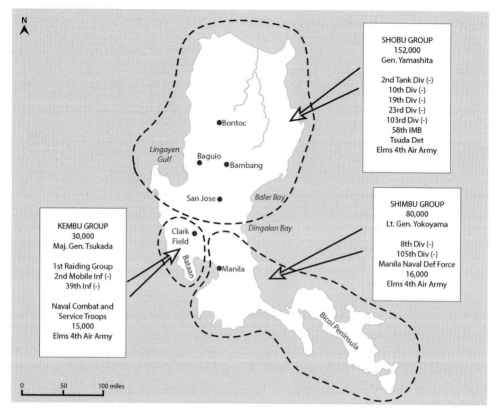

US Army assessment of Japanese forces concentrated in Luzon by 1945.

kept pouring into the Philippines, this put an unbearable strain on food production as the losses to agriculture during the fighting were never replaced. Hence, the prevailing memory of the occupation years for the Filipinos who lived through it were the chronic food shortages and the almost useless 'Mickey Mouse' money distributed to replace outlawed American dollars.

While others preferred to try and sit out the war and perhaps avoid imprisonment, there was no shortage of recruits flocking to join the guerrillas hiding in every corner of the archipelago. These partisans originated from the USAFFE and USAPHIL stragglers who either refused to surrender or escaped captivity. In fact, within weeks of the debacle at Bataan, American soldiers in Northern Luzon had organized cadres of patriots who were willing to undertake any action, be it dangerous or mundane, just so that the war effort was somehow brought to the Japanese. But post-war propaganda has disserviced the Filipino-American guerrilla movement between 1942 and 1945. Rather than crack troops who wiped out entire garrisons of Japanese, the guerrillas preoccupied themselves with intelligence-gathering, relaying any valuable information either by radio or courier involving US Navy submarines prowling Philippine waters, with fresh news and valuable supplies. It wasn't until 1945 when at least two dozen large guerrilla formations consolidated their command structure and fought alongside regular US Army units in Luzon, Visayas and Mindanao. Guerrillas did in fact join the battle of Manila, but their role was limited to helping civilians trapped in the city. Even in combat, the American-led Filipino guerrillas operated like the Soviet partisans, acting as saboteurs of targets of opportunity. "They blew up bridges and mined roads; they blocked supplies to front-line troops; they smashed patrols and ammunition dumps," MacArthur wrote of the loyal guerrillas who fought with him in the Luzon campaign.

The turning point that set the liberation of the Philippines in motion and fulfilled MacArthur's solemn vow took place far away from miserable Luzon. In the summer of 1944, President Franklin D. Roosevelt made a rare trip to the Pacific to confer with his commanders prosecuting the war against Japan. Upon arriving in Pearl Harbor with little fanfare, Roosevelt was briefed on the endgame being readied to smash Tokyo's empire for good. But it was MacArthur, fresh from successive victories in the SWPA, who bucked the prevailing consensus and made an impassioned argument for striking at the Philippines rather than Formosa—the reasoning that the archipelago's airfields, once seized, could help with long-range bomber missions over Japan.

Choosing Formosa over the Philippines was impractical, MacArthur insisted. It was too close for Japanese air and naval reinforcements. He wanted a landing in Mindanao! The available intelligence (supplied by local guerrillas) suggested local defences were patchy at best. There are few credible records detailing what transpired that day at Pearl Harbor when the trajectory of the Pacific War was altered upon MacArthur's relentless pressure. Whatever was said at the conference, Roosevelt was persuaded the most by the fresh ideas on how to win the war sooner rather than later. The SWPA preparations for an assault on the Philippines began in August, with entire divisions ordered to begin training. On 10 October the Fifth Air Force's air campaign started with bomber formations targeting Japanese bases in Formosa and the Philippines. The Fifth's commander, General George C. Kenney, relished the toll his pilots were taking on the enemy. Of course, there were losses to airmen and planes, but at that stage in the war four Japanese aircraft were knocked out for every single American aircraft shot down. To the surprise of SWPA HQ, Kenney's own intelligence-gathering showed ill-prepared Japanese fortifications across the Philippines. A bold stroke was decided upon and on 17 October an armada arrived in the Philippine Sea carrying 100,000 troops protected by a swarm of destroyers and 18 light aircraft carriers with flight decks crowded with planes.

The sudden appearance of such a large invasion fleet near the Visayas, the island cluster in the middle of the Philippine archipelago, threw Tokyo into a panic. The supreme commander of Japanese forces in Southeast Asia, Marshal Hisaichi Terauchi, ordered the naval squadrons refuelling in Brunei and Singapore to proceed with utmost haste toward the Philippine Sea. As many soldiers as could be transported from Luzon were sent to the Visayas and, in a sure sign of desperation, General Tomoyuki Yamashita's own carefully arranged plans for holding the Philippines were neglected. Lionized for his victories in Malaya and Singapore where he humiliated the British, Yamashita arrived at the beginning of the month, probably on 4 October, with clear instructions to repel any American

"I shall return!" On 20 October 1944, General MacArthur and his entourage hit Leyte's Red Beach.

offensive from the SWPA. To keep the Philippines meant the 'island chain' leading to Japan remained impregnable. If the Philippines were lost, the homeland would be in mortal danger from America's vaunted bomber fleet. MacArthur understood this too and together with his staff had drawn up plans for his return to the Philippines under the codename 'Reno'.

Yet Terauchi's attempt to contain the American invasion force proved an utter disaster that sapped the remaining strength of the Japanese army and navy. What became known as the Leyte campaign was a series of battles in and around the island that formed the tenuous backbone to the Philippine archipelago. On 20 October airstrikes and naval bombardment from Halsey's fleet announced the landing of XIV and XXIV Corps. The operation was later immortalized by one of MacArthur's most brazen, if not *the* most brazen, publicity stunt of the war. Wearing aviator glasses and with a corncob pipe clenched between his teeth, MacArthur waded into the ankle-deep water of Red Beach, the designated landing site for the whole operation. Accompanying him were his staff and the late President Quezon's successor, Sergio Osmeña, the acting head of state for the yet-to-be liberated Philippine Commonwealth. MacArthur's presence settled nothing, however, and on 25 October the first wave of A6M Zeroes appeared and smashed into the ships crowded near the shoreline. The anti-aircraft crews were aghast. These weren't torpedo planes but fighters that dived straight for the ships at a distinct angle. When they plunged into the sea their ordnance triggered a geyser dozens of feet high. On that day four escort carriers were hit by the suicide planes, with one sunk.

It was apparent Japan's military aviation, with its losses no longer replenished by active production lines at home, had seized on a novel strategy. Every type of fighter was now a human missile, a *tokkotai*, and its purpose was to inflict as much damage on the Americans who preferred calling them *kamikazes*. The suicide planes were terrifying to behold and the US Navy learned to fear their presence. A whole arsenal was soon released against the Americans, as motor boats were transformed into sea-skimming missiles for knocking out the eggshell transports near the shore and Japanese soldiers revived their *banzai* charges when defeat was imminent. The insanity of fighting to the death soon manifested in every major engagement in the Pacific and climaxed at Manila the following year. But the usefulness of the *kamikazes* in stopping the Americans left much to be desired. Scores of ships were crippled and hundreds killed as a result, but such losses had no lasting effect on operations. The pressure to mount *kamikaze* raids against US Navy vessels meant Japan's overstretched and undersupplied air fleets ended up hastening their decline. By late January 1945 hostile aircraft were absent from the Philippines and regionally. Based on the Fifth Air Force's own records, the Japanese lost 3,000 planes of all types in just several months. In the Philippines alone, several hundred planes were either destroyed in battle or on the ground between October 1944 and January 1945. Almost a thousand cannibalized, damaged or mothballed Japanese fighters were found scattered over Luzon's airfields after the war.

What almost doomed the Leyte campaign were three hair-raising naval engagements, the outcome of which nearly spelled disaster for the Americans. The best known of the three was the battle of Surigao Strait on 23 October, when Rear Admiral Jesse Oldendorf's five battleships 'crossed the T' and decimated the Japanese navy's incoming Southern Force, whose losses totalled three destroyers, two battleships and one cruiser. Meanwhile, as the US infantry divisions on Leyte were preoccupied flushing snipers and machine-gun nests on their march across the island, the warships of the Japanese Central Force were closing in. On the same day when the Leyte amphibious operations were being hyped a success, the Japanese navy's most powerful battleship the INS *Musashi* and its escorts were steaming through the Visayas. If not for the luck of aerial reconnaissance on 24 October, US carrier-based fighter-bombers and torpedo planes would not have set upon the approaching squadron like hornets. In a perverse duel unlike any previous naval encounter in the Pacific, the *Musashi* parried with the buzzing American planes and used its 18-inch main guns against them. Recognized as the largest and most powerful dreadnought ever built, the *Musashi* was the second example of the rare Yamato-class whose expense and scale drained the shipyards responsible for making them. At the height of the encounter, torpedoes managed to damage the *Musashi*'s hull but to little effect. It took 17 direct hits of armor-piercing bombs on its deck and superstructure before the battleship slowed and then lost power. She eventually sank to the bottom due to internal flooding and a thousand sailors went down with her. Two days after the

Musashi's loss in the Sibuyan Sea another formation of Japanese warships rounded Samar island to the north of Leyte and almost caught Halsey's escort carriers off-guard. This was the dreaded Central Force that came very close to terminating the Leyte campaign. But a valiant defence by the available escort carriers and their destroyers discouraged the Japanese fleet from pressing on and it withdrew by evening. Had the Central Force absorbed its losses and fought to the finish, the American invasion fleet would have been scattered and the course of the war in the Pacific changed.

Fighting continued on the island of Leyte until year's end. Between 80,000 and 100,000 Japanese soldiers perished within the same period while a disappointed Terauchi fled to Vietnam, leaving Yamashita to cobble together a workable plan for holding the Philippines as long as possible. Japan's depleted merchant fleet dumped untold tonnage in Manila as confusion reigned in Yamashita's command. The tables had now turned and it was the Japanese who were caught in the same desperate straits as the USAFFE in 1941. In many ways Yamashita's preparations shared remarkable similarities with MacArthur's own flawed approach to territorial defence. Both knew Luzon's size meant no amount of fortifications could secure its long and varied coastline. Like MacArthur three short years before, Yamashita divided his troops into regional clusters. Southern Luzon's dense

The Sixth Army's arrival on the Lingayen beaches on 9 January 1945 met no serious opposition.

forests and mountains were the responsibility of the Shimbu Group. The plains of Central Luzon were under the Kembu Group's purview. Last, Northern Luzon belonged to the Shobu Group led by Yamashita, with its headquarters in Baguio, the same summer capital punished by Japanese bombers on 8 December 1941. As for Manila, Yamashita allowed naval detachments to hold the valuable port and Corregidor. But he wanted the city evacuated as soon as possible. He too realized it was best left to his opponents, who would no doubt spare it.

Recreating the USAFFE's defence of Luzon with the resources available to him in 1945 didn't lead to a different result though. On 9 February another American invasion fleet entered Lingayen Bay unopposed and landed 68,000 troops of the Sixth Army under General Walter Krueger. Like Homma in 1941, Krueger was overly cautious when he considered the logistics of rushing down Central Luzon to reach Manila, an approach that risked a Japanese counterattack from the north or northeast. How strong were Yamashita's divisions, anyway? Krueger's own calculations and the faulty intelligence available to his HQ were muddled. This despite the Sixth Army's overwhelming air superiority and the disorganized resistance it faced—the same advantages Homma's Fourteenth Army had enjoyed. Sixth Army comprised two formations, I Corps under Major General Innis P. Swift and XIV Corps under Major General Oscar Griswold. It was XIV Corps that drove farthest from the Lingayen staging area, its main objectives to secure the main roads

Lieutenant General Walter Krueger, Brigadier General William C. Chase and Major General Innis P. Swift, seen here on Los Negros Island, 1944. (US Army)

leading to Manila as well as critical infrastructure. An important objective was Clark Field at Pampanga where the Far East Air Force used to be based. The 37th Infantry Division, the 'Buckeyes' from Ohio, led by Major General Robert S. Beightler, managed to recapture it after a decisive battle. The CO of the Fifth Air Force arrived to assess the location and had choice words for the Japanese. Seeing the runway littered with abandoned aircraft and equipment, General Kenney wondered how "it was taking so long to defeat so ill-equipped and stupid a nation". Just like Homma's Fourteenth Army in 1941, the Sixth Army in 1945 accomplished most of their objectives in record time, totalling just 12 days from the beach landing at Lingayen to Pampanga.

A fortnight of steady progress was a testament to Sixth Army's cautious momentum in the Luzon campaign. But MacArthur, pressured by a timetable set by the War Department and eager to finish off the Japanese, wanted a rousing arrival in Manila. The arrival of the 1st Cavalry Division led by Major General Verne D. Mudge provided such an opportunity. SWPA HQ knew Yamashita's divisions were scattered in remote areas and lacked the vehicles and motivation for open warfare; the Fifth Air Force did too good a job discouraging them anyway. Recognizing his foe's strategy, MacArthur felt certain Manila was to be abandoned as it had been in his time. Envisioning crowds of Filipinos in the Luneta as infantry columns marched with perfect synchronization, MacArthur insisted Sixth Army make better progress.

But there was another motivation. On 30 January a joint operation involving US Army Rangers and Filipino guerrillas freed hundreds of prisoners trapped at Cabanatuan. This heightened MacArthur's concern for the PoWs he knew were still held by the Japanese. He imagined civilians too—elderly men and mothers with children—were also at the mercy of sadistic Japanese. "The thought of their destruction with deliverance so near was repellent to me," MacArthur confessed in his memoir. A rescue mission was hatched at a last-minute conference with Major General Swing of the 1st Cavalry. As soon as it was finished, Brigadier General William C. Chase was summoned and instructed to lead 'flying columns' bound for Manila. The objective was to reach Santo Tomas and save its occupants as soon as possible. Two squadrons, each 'borrowed' from the 5th and 8th Cavalry Brigades, were readied with attached Shermans from the 44th Tank Battalion, ample motor transport and 105mm howitzer batteries. Once set on course, the flying columns made rapid progress over the northeastern route toward Manila, having few direct encounters with startled Japanese troops.

As per the updated orders from Sixth Army HQ, XIV Corps was supposed to seize the entirety of Manila and its surroundings. This kickstarted a ridiculous competition between the 1st Cavalry's flying columns and the 148th Infantry Regiment of the 37th Infantry Division that quickly descended to farce. The speed of the flying columns over unobstructed roads allowed them to reach Manila in 48 hours without pause. Much to Beightler's disappointment, the 148th was slowed down by damaged bridges and Japanese stragglers. At the very least the 37th Infantry's HQ could take some consolation of being assigned to hold Manila's northern district. If they only knew how terrible the job would turn out.

Major General Robert S. Beightler: National Guardsman

Few commanders in the Luzon campaign suffered as many setbacks as Major General Robert S. Beightler. Having trailed the 1st Cavalry Division during the race to Manila in January, it was his 37th Infantry Division that bore the brunt of the grinding urban combat that lasted till March. Nothing in Beightler's long career prepared him for the tough decisions he needed to make in Manila.

Unlike his peers in Sixth Army, Beightler wasn't a West Point graduate, which always left him uneasy despite his combat experience during World War I and dedication to the Ohio National Guard. When a division of state reservists was activated in October 1940, Beightler's career got

Robert S. Beightler, commander of the 37th Infantry Division, responsible for securing Manila's northwestern approaches.

a final boost with a promotion before the 37th 'Buckeyes,' as they were fondly called, deployed to the Southwest Pacific. This is when he became acquainted with General Oscar Griswold, Sixth Army commander and his direct superior during the Luzon campaign. Surprisingly, the two generals remained friends after the war.

The 37th's first mission for the SWPA had them in Fiji serving as the island's garrison. Brief assignments to Bougainville, New Georgia and Guadalcanal followed. A major Japanese counterattack to recapture Guadalcanal in early 1944 tested Beightler's men but the division held its ground. After a brief period of retraining, the 37th joined Griswold's Sixth Army for the invasion of Luzon via Lingayen on 9 January. Once in the thick of the struggle for Manila, Beightler had no choice but to maximize the firepower against the Japanese who cared little for collateral damage. While it's fair to condemn Beightler's decision for the resulting destructiveness, especially for ordering 155mm and 240mm howitzers to deploy inside the city, the carnage that swept Manila was a consequence of relentless combat between Japanese and American forces and cannot be laid at the feet of a single commander.

The Luzon campaign held a personal connection for Beightler as well: hs son, Robert Jr., was a paratrooper with the 11th Airborne, the division ordered to land in Southern Luzon and take over the Tagaytay highlands. In a rare event in the Pacific theatre, father and son were drawn to the same maelstrom.

Major General Verne D. Mudge: The Lance

No other American division in the Luzon campaign was celebrated like the storied 1st Cavalry owing to Brigadier General Chase's dash for Santo Tomas. But Chase was just following orders from his superior, the elusive Major General Verne D. Mudge, whose leadership of the 1st Cavalry only began in August 1944, barely two months before the division was sent to Leyte. It wasn't until late January when the 1st Cavalry joined the Sixth Army's Luzon campaign—progress of which had so displeased an impatient MacArthur—that Mudge's own career started to spiral upward. Until then his command of the 1st Cavalry had been unremarkable. Still a West Point cadet during World War I, Mudge quietly rose through the ranks for two decades. Once in the thick of Leyte in late 1944, however, he drove his men to fight harder than the unrelenting Japanese. But glimpses of the quirks and personality behind the veneer of Mudge's leadership are rare. His peers in the Southwest Pacific are far more accessible for the newspaper publicity trails and post-retirement literature they left behind.

What started the 1st Cavalry's relentless drive to reach Manila was MacArthur's personal request for Mudge to expedite the rescue of American prisoners trapped in the city. This had untold consequences for the division as its logistics became

Major General Verne D. Mudge (in tank) confers with Brigadier General William C. Chase in Tacloban. (Department of Defense)

overstretched and the flying columns needed round-the-clock air cover by Marine Corps and Fifth Air Force flyers. But the flying columns triggered one of the Luzon campaign's rare comic episodes. Having just retaken Clark Field, Beightler's 37th Infantry relished the idea of fulfilling Manila's heroic liberation. What transpired in the first three days of February 1944 was a race between the 1st Cavalry and the 37th that at times seemed acrimonious—Beightler was known to cuss out his rival upon learning they were ahead of his troops who were bogged down in difficult river crossings. Whether or not the rivalry concealed a personal grudge was never ascertained. But it was the 1st Cavalry who entered Manila first and this proved irresistible to the American press. MacArthur's HQ wanted to bask in the glory as well and declared Manila fully liberated by 7 February, even as entire sections of the city were being razed in the ongoing battle.

The war ended early for Mudge as he relinquished command on 28 February after being wounded by shrapnel from a grenade. Perhaps it was better for him to be replaced. Unlike MacArthur, he didn't have to agonize over what was left of Manila after the fighting was done.

The bodies of three Japanese snipers in a bomb crater, during the fighting on Leyte. (Harry R. Watson / US Coast Guard)

3. DESPERADOES

As Chase's flying columns raced toward Manila, thousands of Japanese troops had failed to withdraw and join the Shimbu Group, or any other formation, that would have spared them from giving battle. This wasn't error however, but absolute defiance in the face of impending catastrophe. With Yamashita having relocated his HQ and the puppet government to Northern Luzon, leaving Manila intact, the prevailing strategy was holding on against the odds. At this point whatever was left of the Japanese army in the Philippines, with its air support gone and logistics in total disarray, was incapable of large-scale offensive operations. But after its near-complete annihilation in Leyte the spectre of ruinous defeat did little to subdue the Japanese navy and its own ground forces. The Manila Naval Defence Force (MNDF) was activated in January by Vice-Admiral Denshichi Okochi on an unspecified date when the army's jurisdiction over the capital expired. But Okochi joined the exodus to Baguio where the Shobu Group was located, sparing itself from the carnage in Central Luzon. By late January it was safe to assume direct contact with Manila was irregular, at best. Okochi did leave a ranking officer in charge of the MNDF, the mysterious Sanji Iwabuchi: his precise rank has never been established by any authoritative text, although he is usually referred to as a rear admiral. His background is just as obscure and it seems he was stationed in the Philippines for a considerable period after a brief tour at Guadalcanal, where he allegedly commanded a warship. No personal artifacts belonging to Iwabuchi survived the war, nor are there any records of

his previous conduct as a naval officer, leaving historians to always ponder his motivations for the sacrilegious bloodshed he let loose on a foreign nation. The sum total of his legacy is a grim photograph whose shadows lend him an eerie visage and an ignoble name forever remembered.

But in 1945 Iwabuchi's MNDF accomplished what Yamashita's HQ could not: a formidable and multilayered defensive plan for holding Manila against whatever the Americans could throw at it. These actions were a fitting bookend for the Japanese's navy's Special Naval Landing Forces, the Rikusentai, who deserve

The only surviving photo of the shadowy Rear Admiral Sanji Iwabuchi.

recognition as Asia's premier marine infantry branch. Unlike their foes in the US Marine Corps, however, Rikusentai were Japanese sailors trained for land warfare and never deployed in numbers greater than a brigade. An intelligence report from 1944 described them as "excellent when unopposed, but when a determined resistance was encountered they exhibited a surprising lack of ability in infantry combat".

Their role during the invasion of Luzon in 1941 was marginal, almost non-existent, and few campaigns in Southeast Asia saw the Rikusentai at the forefront although substantial garrisons were assigned to outposts such as Wake Island and other distant strongholds. The origins of these 'landing troops' are even less distinguished and can be traced to the Russo-Japanese War of 1904, where landing teams of armed sailors fought alongside regular infantry units. The Rikusentai finally emerged as a genuine marine force in the 1930s as Japan sought to impose its will on a weakened China. Their peak was the Second Sino-Japanese War of 1937 when whole battalions fought in Shanghai against the Kuomintang's crack German-trained troops. During World War II, however, the presence of Rikusentai in various battles was almost never acknowledged. One reason for this lapse is their attire and armament was the same as the regular infantry except for the Special Naval Landing Force insignia on their helmets. The years spent

The Japanese Navy's Special Landing Forces, the Rikusentai, during the battle of Shanghai in 1937.

fighting in China may have given the Rikusentai a better grasp of urban warfare compared with regular army units, whose best efforts in the Pacific involved dismal jungle campaigns. With Manila under its thumb, the MNDF likely spent the initial weeks of 1945 amassing weapons and supplies, which arrived until access to Manila Bay was blocked by marauding American aircraft. Indeed, almost no records exist of Japanese merchant vessels or warships abandoned in Manila Bay prior to and during the battle for the city in February.

To allow MNDF commanders greater autonomy, Manila was divided among three formations of varying sizes. Iwabuchi led the Central Force from Intramuros, the walled city that used to be the seat of Spain's colonial regime. The Northern Force controlled the suburbs and the main routes into Manila. The bulk of the17,000-man MNDF was assigned to the vital bases outside the city, Nichols Field and Fort McKinley, entrusted to the control of the Southern Force that held the greatest amount of territory surrounding Manila

This indicates Iwabuchi, along with his superiors, believed a large American force would strike from the south and attempt to retake these bases for immediate use as logistics and command and control facilities. In a final gesture of insubordination, on 27 January, the MNDF HQ informed the Shimbu Group, whose troops were ready to

Soldiers of the Maizuru 1st Special Naval Landing Force are addressed by an officer before the invasion of Hainan, China, 1939. (IJN)

assist with an orderly withdrawal, that Manila was theirs to keep. The brief message read: "The Naval Defence Force will defend its already established positions and crush the enemy's fighting strength."

So began the arduous work of fortifying a city whose previous administration cared more for its amenities than its defences should a siege ever be imposed. Unlike the army that had scattered in various directions over Luzon, the MNDF stockpiled a formidable arsenal. Artillery pieces were brought to Manila and shared out between the three formations. A staggering selection of machine guns was deployed by the MNDF, probably cannibalized from the disabled aircraft abandoned at Nichols Field.

By late January 1945 the MNDF had succeeded in concentrating its manpower at specific locations. Iwabuchi still anticipated an offensive from Southern Luzon, the goal of which was to reach Dewey Boulevard and encircle Manila. As a contingency, each of the bridges over the Pasig river was readied for demolition, but it seems the frantic preparations of the Rikusentai were half-baked at best. The jeeps and tanks of Chase's flying columns reached Grace Park at noon on 3 February. The Bonifacio Monument, a stirring pedestal of Italian bronze and German marble dedicated to the revolutionary hero, welcomed the 1st Cavalry Division's vanguard. But so did the Japanese. Gunfire rang out from nearby buildings and the tanks were soon blasting away at close range as they made inexorable progress toward Manila proper. Oddly, neither physical obstructions nor booby traps had been prepared to anticipate the sudden arrival of an American mechanized column. But it was evening before the Shermans of the 44th found Santo Tomas and crashed through its main gate. Far from a joyous entrance, the hour of arrival and the fearful internees huddled within their barracks didn't make for a climactic occasion. The prisoners had had reason to hope since an aviator flying reconnaissance had swept above Santo Tomas and relinquished his goggles where he had tucked a handwritten note—help was on the way! On the tense evening when it did, confusion ensued as the sentries, who were later identified as Formosan conscripts, either fled or surrendered to an uncertain fate. Luckily, there was no last-ditch stand to imperil the lives of those trapped in Santo Tomas, while the tanks idled in place. However, the cavalrymen soon had to contend with a devious opponent. Rather than give battle, Lieutenant Colonel Toshio Hayashi instructed his men to retreat inside one of the colleges and take as many hostages with them. This was the first definitive scene of Japanese perfidy in Manila. Almost 300 women and children were forced to act as human shields around Hayashi's troops. The living conditions inside Santo Tomas were little better than a slum and multiple cases of starvation deaths were already accounted for by the internees. To worsen their plight in the hour of deliverance, there was now a full-blown hostage situation on campus. The standoff was not resolved by morning when the rest of Chase's flying column arrived and were skirmishing with Rikusentai as they tried to reach the Pasig river. Hayashi's troops won their freedom with an honour-bound agreement they would not be fired upon. In a final display of bravado, the Japanese formed a column and marched out of Santo Tomas with their weapons. The gesture may have been defiant to the core but what fate awaited Hayashi's men was never discovered. On the day of their negotiated relief the unit had an equal chance of being

A Rikusentai strongpoint. (Navy Ministry of Japan)

slaughtered by the guerrillas who had trailed the flying columns, or perhaps these same troops dispersed and surrendered later on. But there was little relief for the internees as mortars soon began landing on campus, injuring dozens, in a clear signal the Japanese holding Manila had no regard for civilians. This only added to the overwhelming distress of the former prisoners. Among the women, malnutrition had caused their hair to fall out when they combed it. For the children, the GIs' rations and canned fruit juice were a feast, a welcome alternative to the soggy gruel they had endured for months and years. Rather than evacuate the 3,700 internees, the men of the 1st Cavalry welcomed the Red Cross. After three years of captivity the first ecstatic telegrams from America brought fresh tears and euphoric relief to the families who had been torn from the world by their imprisonment.

The last thing the Santo Tomas internees expected was MacArthur himself to show up in the next few days just when the fighting around Manila was becoming more intense. Received like a Hollywood movie star, the SWPA commander's presence elicited simultaneous tears and jubilation. MacArthur being MacArthur, however, just as at Leyte's Red Beach, the moment deserved a bold declaration for the sake of the papers back home. On 7 February his staff circulated his official announcement of Manila's liberation even as Beightler's 37th Infantry was mired in house-to-house fighting and the three main bridges over the Pasig river had been blown. Here was the MacArthur Paradox in full display, an upsetting mix of boundless optimism and hype just when the tactical situation was becoming uncontrollable. While MacArthur's sentiments toward the Philippines and its people were genuine, his blatant missteps—the failure to anticipate Japan's invasion of the Commonwealth, for example—led to dire consequences that he had never reckoned with.

The 1st Cavalry's sudden arrival in Manila may have caught the Japanese off guard for a short interval but a single, sudden incident ultimately dashed whatever optimism the men in the flying columns had for a clean victory. Not wishing to dissipate the momentum, Chase's jeeps quit the bedlam at Santo Tomas for the Luneta farther south. Just a quick drive until the Quezon bridge over the Pasig and the Americans would reach the administrative centre of Manila. Yet before they reached the nearest corner, machine guns chattered from the Far Eastern University, where the Rikusentai had been holed up all along, no doubt aware of the Americans' arrival and waiting for them to materialize. The volume of fire discouraged any further movement on the street as the 1st Cavalry faced a rude introduction to the weeks ahead.

A distinctive newspaperman's spin applied to the battle of Manila was to fashion its tribulations as "The Warsaw of the East". But there was little to compare aside from the prevailing destruction in both cities. No great revolt or patriotic rising swept Manila in 1945 as the Sixth Army came nearer and nearer. While some daring residents managed to escape when Yamashita ordered his HQ out of the city, the MNDF's preparations left almost a million residents trapped in their homes. Movement anywhere was dangerous as tense sentries enforced a curfew. While guerrillas mobilized in the provinces, ready to

Two North American A-27s of the 17th Pursuit Squadron at Nichols Field, Philippines, in 1941. (USAF)

A portrait of Brigadier General Vicente Lim, by Vicente Manansala.

harass the Japanese, no great intrigues were afoot in Manila. Even the finest soldier in the Commonwealth, the West Point alumnus General Vicente Lim, submitted to imprisonment without protest. The former commander of the 41st Philippine Division, an all-Filipino formation that distinguished itself in Bataan, was jailed in the Bilibid complex under suspicion of meeting local spies. His remains were never found. Lim's disappearance at the hands of his captors formed a greater ordeal for so many Filipinos as the occupation neared its end: a ruthless crackdown had swept Manila since the beginning of the fighting in Leyte that broke the city's spirit. Among the multitude of victims was Vicente Singson, Jr., the eldest son of a local tycoon who had served in the American colonial government before the Commonwealth. Condemned to Fort Santiago on trumped-up charges, nearly three months of beatings and confinement had left him emaciated and deaf in one ear. Upon his release, he remained bedridden in his Singson home just a short drive from the miseries of Santo Tomas. With his brothers having joined the guerrillas, left to care for him was his sister Nieves, only recently married the year before.[*]

---

[*] Nieves was the author's grandmother.

Above: The Santa Cruz bridge, still intact before the battle.

Below: Dewey Boulevard (now Roxas Boulevard) and Luneta, prior to February 1945.

Above: Aerial view of Bilibid Prison.

Below: A Japanese Mogami-class cruiser, most probably the *Kumano*, under attack by USN Carrier Air Group 7 (CVG-7) following the Battle of Leyte Gulf, 26 October 1944. A Curtiss SB2C-3 Helldiver of Bombing Squadron 7 (VB-7) is visible in the upper right of the photograph. (US Navy)

Above: USS *Pennsylvania* BB-38 firing on Leyte. (World War II History Org)

Right: Filipino volunteers carry supplies into the mountains to reach 1st Cavalry Division troops in the battle of Leyte. (NARA / ibiblio.org)

Above: USS *Cony* (DD-508) lays a smoke screen off Leyte on 20 October 1944. (US Navy)

Below: The invasion of Leyte. (National Archives, Navy 80-G-258487)

Above: Landing barges sweep toward the beaches of Leyte Island as American and Japanese aircraft dog-fight above. (US Coast Guard)

Below: Douglas MacArthur inspecting the beachhead on Leyte Island. (US National Archives)

Above: The 7th Cavalry Regiment moves inland off the Leyte beachhead, 20 October 1944.

Left: A Filipino woman carries the family cross to safety, Leyte, 6 November 1944.

Above: Filipino women pick their way through the smoldering village of Dulag. (Associated Press via John Tewell)

Right: Ruperto Kangleon reporting to General Douglas MacArthur during ceremonies proclaiming the liberation of Leyte, 23 October 1944. Kangleon would serve as Secretary of National Defense under the Roxas administration. (Department of The Navy: Naval Historical Center)

Above: Vice-Admiral Thomas C. Kinkaid, USN, Commander Seventh Fleet, watches landing operations in Lingayen Gulf, Leyte, from the bridge of his flagship, USS *Wasatch* (AGC-9), circa 9 January 1945.(US Navy / NARA)

Below: A US Navy Curtiss SB2C-3 Helldiver of Bombing Squadron VB-7 in flight over ships of Task Force 38. VB-7 operated from the aircraft carrier USS *Hancock* (CV-19) during the period from September 1944 to January 1945, and that participated in the battle of Leyte Gulf in October 1944. A Grumman F6F-5 Hellcat from Fighting Squadron VF-7 is visible in the background. (US Navy)

4. THE ANGELS

Mere days before the liberation of Santo Tomas another daring endeavour, undertaken on a much larger scale, took place nearly a hundred kilometres south. The 11th Airborne Division was shipped from Leyte to the shores of Nasugbu and tasked with penetrating deep into Japanese lines. What Eighth Army HQ dubbed Operation Mike VI was a tad ambiguous—an elaborate reconnaissance involving an entire division sent to wrest rugged terrain without a proper assessment of enemy strength. Arriving in Manila was deemed a possibility.

Before the ensuing events are explained, it is important to establish the role of the 11th Airborne. The Angels, a moniker inspired by the division's patch, were created in February 1943 at North Carolina's Camp Mackall where 12,000 green recruits spent months training to become paratroopers. Their commander, Major General Joseph Swing, was a career army man who had never dabbled in any 'airborne' theorizing. Aside from a spell of combat in World War I, Swing spent two decades passing on his howitzer expertise. Oddly, the several months of toil in North Carolina earned the Angels a deployment far away from Europe, where the US Army's airborne divisions were performing critical roles. Delivered by train to San Francisco and marched into sweltering troopships, the Angels sailed across the Pacific, reaching Papua New Guinea in July 1944. The voyage itself was an ordeal. As a precaution during ocean crossings, troop convoys had to button up at night. This meant all hatches were closed so that lamps and other illumination would not attract enemy attention. Of course, the occupants were condemned to sweat in their miserable bunks, almost choking from the humidity. Soldiers coped by moving onto the deck at night where the cool air chilled their tired forms and by daytime mass calisthenics and numbing drills helped stave off boredom.

By the time they arrived in Papua, the Angels had little to do except guard a vital airstrip at Dobodura and continue their training. At peak strength the division totalled 12,700 men divided between the 511th, 674th and 675th Parachute Infantry Regiments and the 187th and 188th Glider Infantry Regiments. The sojourn at Dobodura was memorable for its warm climate and passable food (canned meat and potatoes) with highlights provided by rare USO (United Service Organizations) shows.

It wasn't until mid-November when the whole division was ordered to Leyte that the division saw combat. However, rather than utilize their skills as paratroopers, upon landing in Bitu Beach on 18 November, Swing's troops were treated like a regular infantry albeit with a startling lack of motor transport, a disadvantage that would haunt them in Luzon. The Angels spent the rest of 1944 trekking over rain-sodden jungle as they clashed with Japanese remnants holding out in Leyte's mountainous interior where the mud and muck stuck everywhere and the men referred to themselves as mud rats. By Christmas the division was ensconced in the northeast of the island guarding another airstrip. The pause in combat meant diversions such as sunbathing and outdoor movies at night.

But rumours of an operation in Luzon swirled. Orders eventually arrived in mid-January, settling weeks of anticipation. The Angels were to land at Nasugbu and march until they reached the Tagaytay highlands where the 511th would be dropped by air. Although the primary objective was to ascertain the extent of Japanese defences, MacArthur's HQ made it clear that the Eighth Army could deploy the Angels north toward Manila should the opportunity present itself.

Located to the distant southwest of Manila where the terrain and infrastructure were less accessible, it might have seemed wiser had a few divisions seized Bicol instead, where even longer stretches of unguarded beaches lay waiting. Bicol was closer to Leyte and formed the 'tail' of Luzon with its volcanic peaks and scenic hills. It also made better sense from the standpoint of air power. All throughout January American troops noticed the remarkable absence of Japanese aircraft and those frightful kamikazes, so much so

General MacArthur and Lieutenant General Eichelberger at Rockhampton, Australia, in 1943. (State Library of Queensland)

that Eighth Army HQ tried arranging an airdrop for the 11th Airborne over Central Luzon but logistics proved inadequate. Another idea was combining three divisions for a landing in Southern Luzon but once again the lack of transports deemed it unfeasible. So expediency dictated Nasugbu for a scaled-down amphibious landing. No doubt, a serious consideration was Highway 17, also known as Route 17, a winding two-lane road that traced a path over the Tagaytay highlands all the way to Cavite and then on to Manila. Yet no amount of air reconnaissance could ascertain any enemy presence. Eighth Army HQ's best intelligence guessed 50,000 Japanese were occupying the town with networks of trenches dug all the way to Tagaytay. Would it be too difficult for an amphibious assault on Manila Bay, whether at Cavite or Bataan, just as the Sixth Army swept into the capital? Indeed, XI Corps was preparing to land along Bataan's eastern edge. As for a direct assault on Manila Bay, this was adjudged too risky because the chances of Japanese aircraft and layered coastal defences suggested it would prove a bloodbath. Once again, Nasugbu was an optimum choice: close enough to the main objective when pinpointed on a map yet far enough from any large Japanese force—probably.

After a series of mock amphibious landings in Leyte, the Angels boarded transports commanded by Rear Admiral William Fletcher. Accompanying them was Eighth Army HQ, i.e. General Robert Eichelberger and his staff. It took five days to reach their destination.

Lieutenant General Robert Eichelberger. (1 Lt G. A. Stevens / US Army Signal Corps)

The 511th, however, was flown to Mindoro, a mountainous island used as a logistical hub by the Fifth Air Force, where they awaited the crucial order to jump. On the morning of X-Day or 31 January a fleet of 50 transports escorted by destroyers reached Nasugbu. Once the preparatory bombardment from the destroyers ceased, the Japanese remained unseen and unheard. The landing craft carrying three regiments of the 11th Airborne sailed over placid waters unthreatened by suicide planes or torpedo boats; neither were mines or Japanese coastal guns in evidence. Nasugbu was unspoiled and waiting. From their landing ships the troops would have spied the distant beach like a golden thread running below a carpet of jungle greenery. Even the sea posed no difficulties as waves rolled gently shoreward.

Perfect timing was on the side of Swing's Angels as the Nasugbu landing on the designated Red Beach commenced with no serious resistance. The morning's great headache was a sandbar preventing the transports carrying the vehicles from reaching the beach. Minor hostilities did break out with the sudden chatter of machine guns from concealment but this had little effect on the Angels' progress from Red Beach to the town proper. When the 188th Parachute Infantry Regiment arrived in Nasugbu, rather than a rude awakening from the Japanese, the overjoyed Filipinos welcomed them with open arms. Even General Eichelberger was impressed by the reception. In his post-war memoir he recalled "the only town of any consequence we had seen in the Pacific ... Filipinos lined the streets and gave away such precious hoarded food stocks as eggs, chickens, bananas, papayas. There was a village square and bandstand, a lot of cheering and chatter."

On the first day of Operation Mark VI the only significant event was capturing a sugarcane plantation where a pint-sized locomotive delighted the troops who used it as a tram for hauling supplies. Such agricultural enterprises were common across Luzon and the Visayas as Philippine sugar had been a vital export in the pre-war years. So lucrative was the commodity, in fact, that vast fortunes afforded enviable lifestyles and palatial manors for the elite families who owned the plantations. For the Japanese to have not set the Nasugbu sugarcane ablaze or, as the Americans feared, blown up its infrastructure was fortunate. At least some vestige of peacetime could still be put to good use once the national economy was up and running again.

Within 48 hours the majority of 11th Airborne was ashore. Swing established his divisional HQ at the Palico Barracks, a site named after the river it was meant to protect, and from where he could observe his troops' progress in securing the vital Route 17. It mattered for the Angels to march unimpeded. As soon as they reached the highlands, the 511th Parachute Infantry Regiment and its attachments, also known as the Regimental Combat Team or RCT, were to be dropped over Tagaytay Ridge overlooking the picturesque Taal Lake. The rest of 11th Airborne was expected to link up with the 511th once on the ground and drive north until they reached Cavite, whence they could make a dash for Nichols Field and then Fort McKinley, the two vital military bases outside the Philippine capital.

To grasp the significance of an airborne operation over Tagaytay Ridge, its geography deserves a brief aside. Formed by an ancient crater left by a volcanic eruption that occurred

Tagaytay Ridge with Mount Sungay as seen from Santo Tomas, Batangas. (Ramon F. Velasquez)

in distant millennia, what became known as Tagaytay—the etymology of the name is unclear—was uninhabited until the American colonial era and the Commonwealth. There were neither plantations nor settlements in Tagaytay, as if its distance from the coast discouraged any development. It also formed part of the Tagalog region of Southern Luzon where the revolution against Spain began almost half a century prior. Rather than an ethnicity, the Tagalogs were the industrious lowland farmers and fisherfolk who bore the brunt of colonization and were always at odds with the neighbouring Pampangueños of Pampanga from Central Luzon who spoke their own distinct language. So vital was the role of the Tagalog-speaking Filipinos in the struggle for freedom that the national language, as decreed by President Quezon, was to be the Pilipino spoken by the Tagalogs. Indeed, the inclusiveness of Filipino nationalism is somewhat diminished by the Tagalog language's primacy. Deemed a worthwhile tourist spot for its majestic view of Taal Lake, the surface of which was like a giant mirror surrounding the volcanic islet at its centre shaped like a teardrop, no less than President Quezon hailed the establishment of a sumptuous hotel with an adjacent golf course built over a ridge with a splendid wind-swept view.* The venue, which was managed as an extension of the fabled Manila Hotel

---

* The same building remains open for business today as the Taal Vista Hotel

so loved by well-heeled Americans, could only be reached by car on a single road that sliced through acres upon acres of farmland and forest until the steep incline up toward Tagaytay. Undeterred by its remoteness, wealthy families and even holy orders rushed to build their own well-appointed getaways in Tagaytay, whose territorial limits were used as the boundaries for a municipality of the same name established via presidential decree. None of this mattered to Eighth Army's HQ in 1945, but Tagaytay's single road connecting with Manila was of such grave importance and the best plan for taking it was by dropping an entire regiment on a steep ridge in broad daylight.

The urgency of reaching Tagaytay Ridge initiated the first and only decisive battle the Angels fought before they reached Manila. Route 17 ran between a narrow pass overshadowed by three peaks that rose thousands of feet above sea level: Aiming, Batulao and Cariliao. It was expected that the Japanese defenders had dug in for a protracted fight. This early assessment proved true and up against the 11th Airborne's spearhead from Nasugbu, led by the 188th, was the so-called Fuji Force, an independent formation led by a mere colonel, that enjoyed the high ground and had gun emplacements prepared for blocking the Americans. Enormous ditches had also been excavated at three points on the highway to serve as tank traps. Although encouraged by the light resistance of 31 January,

The 11th fought like a regular infantry division during the mud- and rain-soaked Leyte campaign.

Instead of stiff Japanese resistance, cheering crowds greeted the Angels' arrival in Luzon.

Swing and his staff were unaware of how strong the Japanese ahead of them were. In fact, the bulk of the Fuji Force had deliberately vacated Nasugbu to concentrate its strength, which comprised a battered infantry division and stragglers from a suicide boat unit, at the Aiming–Batulao–Cariliao junction. On the morning of 1 February, with the Angels having seized Palico bridge with such haste that the Japanese demolition team readying charges had fled at the sight of Americans, the 188th's forward elements came under fire as they attempted to reach Tagaytay proper.

Undeterred, the 188th did its best to secure the mountains. Their primary advantage was the Fifth Air Force from Mindoro which hammered at the Japanese without pause while a single company marched up Mount Aiming and cleared its heights. This was necessary so that concentrated fire could be directed at the Japanese on Batulao and Cariliao. The men of A Company held fast as Japanese infantry tried in vain to dislodge them. In yet another instance where Japanese airpower showed itself to be almost non-existent, no fighters from Clark or Nichols appeared. As far as Eighth Army's Eichelberger was concerned, he judged the Mindoro-based US fighter-bombers "decisive" and "heartening" as they helped clear the Japanese from Mount Aiming. What did slow the Angels, however, were the jungle-covered heights of the other two mountains. The division's

75mm pack howitzers were inadequate against the fearsome 105mm and 120mm artillery pieces the Japanese had emplaced in impenetrable tree cover. The best course of action for the battalion and company COs was to deploy their men slowly around the enemy flanks as mortars plastered the Japanese as best as they could. This is what decided the battle as a single battalion of the 188th ascended Cariliao on 2 February and routed the defenders. To the surprise of the Americans, some Japanese held on until the following morning when the 187th leapfrogged the 188th to reach Tagaytay. The last serious resistance at the peaks dragged through the afternoon and evening and into the morning on 3 February.

Ever since their arrival in Nasugbu, the Angels had moved on foot: the progress they made between 31 January and 2 February was remarkable. A clever stratagem encouraged by Eighth Army HQ was to send the few jeeps and trucks of the division's motor pool thundering down Route 17, to give the impression of an entire army on the move from the Nasugbu beaches, which Eighth Army hoped would demoralize the Fuji Force. In another startling turn, once Japanese resistance crumbled at the Aiming–Batulao–Cariliao junction, the 188th swept into the *barrio* of Aga below Mount Aiming where they discovered the Fuji Force command post. To their surprise, the Japanese had vacated the position without booby trapping it, leaving behind immense quantities of ordnance. It was clear the Fuji Force was supposed to stop 11th Airborne dead in its tracks but what transpired instead was a farcical defence that neither bloodied nor halted the Angels' progress. Eighth Army HQ did not spare its praise. "The troops stood up unflinchingly under artillery fire and performed flawlessly," Eichelberger recalled. "In 28 hours ashore they had advanced 18 miles on foot. All combat equipment was unloaded, a port and an airstrip were established [in Nasugbu]."

Indeed, the dismal performance of the Fuji Force in Southern Luzon more than echoed the USAFFE's own bungling performance in December 1941 against General Homma. It revealed serious weaknesses in the Japanese army at large. Here was a well-supplied Japanese formation assigned to defend an area with abundant natural barriers. But in a matter of days its best efforts proved wanting as an under-equipped American division managed to overcome its carefully prepared defences with minimal casualties. With the benefit of hindsight, Operation Mike VI exposed at least three glaring weaknesses in the Japanese at the time. First was their shabby logistics. From the start of the Nasugbu landings until the crossing at Palico, the Fuji Force had withdrawn to Route 17 and concentrated its defences in a single location that also held its supplies. A second and equally disappointing weakness was the lack of air support. Whereas the Japanese divisions sent to Leyte in late 1944 had the benefit of robust, albeit doomed, fighter cover, by the time the 11th Airborne arrived in Southern Luzon this no longer existed. Neither could marine or aviation suicide attacks be counted on to demoralize the Americans. Third, and last, the brief existence of the Fuji Force and their ultimate defeat meant that Japanese tactics, and even their equipment, were inferior when compared to the US Army's. The defenders at Nasugbu and Mount Cariliao had bigger and more plentiful weapons than the 11th Airborne, an understrength division of lightly armed paratroopers on foot and without tank or heavy artillery support, yet the Japanese arsenal at Route 17 turned out to be inadequate. The evidence from Central Luzon and the rapid collapse of the Fuji Force suggested Yamashita's best-laid plans for holding out against MacArthur were as badly put together as the USAFFE's.

As the Aiming–Batulao–Cariliao junction was subdued, the 187th was almost stopped cold at the highest point on Tagaytay Ridge where the Fuji Force had another network of fortifications, albeit on a smaller scale. What the Angels dubbed Shorty Ridge—named after Colonel 'Shorty' Soule who led the 188th—was a frustrating impediment that threatened the delicate timetable imposed on Swing and his paratroopers. If Tagaytay Ridge wasn't secured for the oncoming 511th then additional time would have to be spent concentrating the division's resources for an offensive against the Japanese, which in turn would afford more time for Yamashita's Shimbu Group and the Japanese garrison in Manila. Still, the orders arrived for the 511th to do their part.

At 0815 on 3 February two waves of C-47 transports from Mindoro delivered the 511th to Tagaytay Ridge. The bare landing zone had previously been reconnoitred by a Pathfinder unit on foot. The flight path of the C-47s traced the eastern half of Taal Lake before it swept in low for the drop. Jumping over Tagaytay had its risks. While the tree cover on the ridge was sparse, a powerful gust of biting wind could hurl a paratrooper away from the drop zone and send him tumbling down a rugged slope that reached down to the lake shore. Falling into Taal Lake wasn't a pleasant thought either. But when the Angels leapt from their planes that morning, in the largest airborne operation undertaken by the division to date and, in what was surely disappointing for Swing, it went almost completely awry as the 511th miscalculated their timing despite the absence of enemy fire. In a matter of hours, 1,325 GIs floated down to Tagaytay but only a quarter ended up in the right place. Several hundred touched ground miles away and the entire effort would have been a debacle had the Japanese fortified Tagaytay Ridge sufficiently. This egregious scattering of paratroopers is an overlooked mishap in the unit's history and is omitted from the few official records that survive today. The 11th Airborne almost botched its toughest assignment in the Philippines after months of being deployed as de facto marine infantry storming out of landing ships. But the Angels' luck held at Tagaytay Ridge and only one paratrooper was killed, in an accident. Meanwhile, Swing and the rest of the Eighth Army brass later relocated to the "Manila Hotel Annex", their designation for the Commonwealth-era Taal Vista Lodge. By noon on 3 February the Angels had sufficiently pummelled Shorty Ridge with air power and artillery to reduce the position to irrelevance, killing some 300 Japanese in the process. The last gasp of Japanese resistance was responsible for a tense encounter that put the Eighth Army's leadership in harm's way. Eager to observe his men in action, Swing arrived at Tagaytay to catch the 188th and 187th mopping up the last defenders. Unfortunately, he was accompanied by Eichelberger and his staff, who were all intent on observing the battle themselves. In one frightful instance, a hail of mortars pinned the senior officers behind cover. The Eighth Army almost lost its commander when shrapnel tore into Eichelberger's aide-de-camp and left Colonel Soule of the 188th injured. Colonel Coe was killed, Colonel Wilson and Captain Lyman of the 187th were wounded. "I watched a doctor dig the slug out of [Colonel Robert] Soule and fill the hole with iodine," Eichelberger recalled. "Then I saw Soule take off through the high, coarse grass to cheer on his troops to the conquest of Tagaytay Ridge."

Time was of the essence. With the 11th Airborne almost at full strength, the 511th was assigned a small collection of trucks and ordered to Manila at full speed, just as planned if the operation was to meet its schedule. The moment of their departure was particularly dramatic as the troops on Tagaytay Ridge gazed down on the capital below. As night fell over Manila thick smoke tinged with orange fire rising from Tondo drove home the horrors awaiting them. Swing knew his division was overstretched and would be at a disadvantage in a pitched battle. Never mind the worrisome logistical pinch as 11th Airborne's supplies, including desperately soon-to-be-needed medical kits, had to travel dozens of miles, from Nasugbu to Tagaytay, and then farther still to their final objective of Manila. But MacArthur ordered the southern approaches to the capital sealed. On the same night that whole sections of Manila burned, the 511th rumbled toward the Genko Line. The Angels were about to face their toughest challenge.

Infantry cautiously move toward an enemy machine-gun on Leyte, Philippines, late 1944. (ibiblio.org)

Major General Joseph May Swing: The Archangel

An atypical commander of an unortho-dox division, like his peers in the US Army, Joseph May Swing was a West Point alumnus who fought in the Great War and spent the following decades crawling up the ranks as an artillery instructor. Pearl Harbor did him no favors and, still a mere colonel, it seemed like the War Department had better use for him behind a desk rather than leading men in combat. But once assigned to the 11th Airborne, Swing's enthusiasm for gruelling forced marches and meticulous planning whipped the Angels into shape. It all paid off at Leyte, where the 11th went up against desperate Japanese resistance.

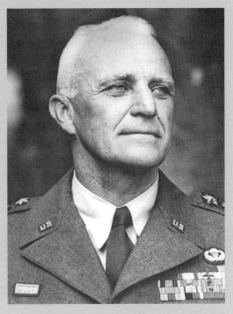

Despite the odds facing his men, General Swing never lost his composure.

As part of Eichelberger's Eighth Army, in January 1945 Swing's Angels were tasked with opening the Luzon campaign from the south with an elaborate multi-pronged operation in the Batangas highlands. Although Swing's troops proved resilient, tough and unwavering in pursuit of their objectives, the Angels had the darndest luck among the divisions that fought in Luzon. During the battle of Manila, the Angels weren't just pressed for time—they had to race toward the capital at all cost—but the scope of their responsibilities were far greater than other Sixth Army divisions—the 1st Cavalry and 37th Infantry—thundering down from Central Luzon. Swing's men had to close the southern outskirts of Manila and retake the two vital military installations held by the MNDF's best-equipped units.

The Angels also distinguished themselves in the flawless raid on Los Baños, where thousands of civilian PoW's were being held, and continued rolling back Yamashita's stragglers in Southern Luzon until the war's end. During one particu-lar engagement in April, Swing showed he was every bit as tough as the young men under his command when he took charge of a tank destroyer unit on foot, hollering orders by radio. He then led his own troops to overwhelm a Japanese position. Swing's decisiveness earned him a Distinguished Service Cross.

After garrison duty in Japan and the Korean War, Swing's retirement from the army paved the way to a full-time role as the head of a federal agency in the 1950s, the Eisenhower era. He died aged 89 on 9 December 1984.

5. ENCIRCLEMENT

With the battle of Manila having begun in earnest and the bridges over the Pasig river destroyed, the XIV Corps had to adjust its strategy. For the 37th Infantry Division, consolidating its side of the Pasig was paramount. The 1st Cavalry Division, on the other hand, had a more strenuous task: securing the utilities outside Manila. Their primary objective was the Novaliches dam farther east. As for the 11th Airborne, they were still travelling down from the Tagaytay highlands, heading straight for Nichols Field in Manila's southern extremities.

To Griswold's disappointment, the XIV Corps divisions encountered innumerable difficulties as a result of not knowing the extent of Japanese defences around the city. Just as the 1st Cavalry Division's flying column was frustrated on their way to Quezon bridge on 4 February, which was demolished and rendered unusable, so did the 37th Infantry Division taste failure when the Jones and Santa Cruz bridges met the same fate, cutting off any direct access to Intramuros. But there was still reason for optimism. With the 1st Cavalry Division giving Manila proper a wide berth, the 37th Infantry Division set about clearing their sector of Japanese troops. Actionable intelligence a day after the fateful liberation of Santo Tomas revealed more PoWs were being held at the colonial-era Bilibid Prison, which was next to the Far Eastern University that had given the flying columns so much grief earlier.

Undeterred, the university was cleared in a matter of hours and another rescue effected on Bilibid whose 'wagon wheel' layout attested to its 19th-century origins. The 148th Infantry Regiment found 1,350 prisoners inside, a population divided between PoWs and civilian expatriates. But there was no reason to celebrate yet, since three more objectives awaited. These were the neighbourhoods of Binondo, Escolta and Tondo, on the northwestern edge of the city facing Intramuros and representing the Commonwealth's main commercial district. If governance was centralized in the administrative buildings surrounding Luneta, the national economy was run from the offices and warehouses that crowded the real estate the 37th Infantry Division had to liberate.

The Escolta was particularly strategic. More than a premium address for businesses and boutiques, either end of this historic street was connected to the Jones and Santa Cruz bridges. To control it offered an uninterrupted view of Intramuros and the grandiose Post Office with its majestic columns mirrored by the Pasig river flowing beneath. In the final decades of the Spanish colonial era, British merchant banks lined either side of the Escolta while imported wares from Europe to Japan arriving by sea were either sold in Binondo, a ghetto reserved for Chinese labourers, or stored in the Tondo warehouses. Of course, under American colonial rule new influences reshaped these colourful neighbourhoods. Neon signs plastered the Escolta and horse-drawn buggies clattered over its

The internees liberated by the 1st Cavalry in Santo Tomas and Bilibid were immediately provided food, medicine and new clothes.

scenic length alongside chauffeured cars. Binondo flourished with cinemas and restaurants, eventually being recognized as Manila's very own 'Chinatown' while Tondo kept its role as a maze-like sprawl of warehouses for the cargo unloaded at the North and South Port Areas. By February 1945, however, the area was held by the MNDF's Northern Force with explicit orders to resist for as long as possible.

The struggle for Binondo and Tondo began in earnest after Bilibid's liberation. Encountering stiff resistance, the 37th's divisional artillery was brought in to hasten the job but as the day wore on it became apparent the Japanese were far more numerous and determined than expected. Unknown to Beightler and his commanders on the ground, as evening set on 4 February, the Northern Force managed a clean withdrawal aided by selective demolitions in Tondo that gutted building after building. Much of the following day was spent trying to mobilize local firemen and contain the inferno. But the destruction of Tondo wiped any hope that seizing Manila could be done quickly. Since the 1st Cavalry Division's flying columns rushed to Santo Tomas on 3 February, the ensuing week was a parade of disappointments that, with the arrival of artillery and subsequent destruction visited on Tondo, set the pattern for the days ahead.

American firepower

As the flying columns of the 1st Cavalry Division linked up with the 37th Infantry Division in Manila's northern suburbs, the heavy resistance around Tondo and the North Port Area served as a rude awakening for the Sixth Army, whose HQ fancied an uneventful 'liberation' attended by ecstatic crowds. On the contrary, the moment the Americans reached Grace Park the initial skirmishing dimmed any prospects for an easy conquest. In the days following the relief of Santo Tomas, a new stratagem was put together by XIV Corps that involved dedicated urban warfare. For lack of better options, given MacArthur's orders forbidding airstrikes against the city he once called home, the commanders of the 1st Cavalry Division and the 37th Infantry Division were given free reign with the weapons they had as long as they did their best to avoid indiscriminate fire on civilians.

But the Rikusentai defending Manila had a formidable arsenal of their own. Predictably, the fighting that commenced across the northeastern outskirts and suburbs of Manila in early February was catastrophic. The extent of Japanese fortifications, where every large building was held by infantry armed with machine guns and sometimes anti-aircraft pieces used at close range in a ground role, meant the Americans had to respond in kind. Unlike 1942, the average GI had a greater selection of portable weapons at his disposal and could depend on overwhelming support from armour and the self-propelled mounts—howitzers and tank destroyers—that excelled in softening up the opposition. As Japanese resistance proved increasingly stubborn, the greater the volume of ordnance unleashed on them.

XIV Corps brought their 155mm 'Long Toms' inside Manila to crush the remaining defenders.

Above: The 37th Infantry Division's 240mm artillery was used to smash the walls of Intramuros.

Below: US 75mm howitzers were extremely potent at close range.

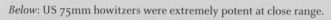

It is important to dwell a little on what the destruction of Tondo meant for Manila's desperate inhabitants. In the wake of the fire a terrible social experiment was now forced on those left newly homeless. How were they to manage while the Americans busied themselves with liberating Manila from the stubborn Japanese? By whatever means necessary, it turned out. After the war, Binondo and Escolta managed to regain some of their former glory but a new culture arose in Tondo—the eternal slum for Manila's downtrodden, the squatters. In the messy post-war reconstruction Tondo was reborn as a den of iniquity and vice. It remains an eyesore to this day, better known for its shoddy public housing and trash heaps rather than the vital role it once upheld for the national economy. Forgotten by *Manileños*, who are all too famil-iar with the persistence of slums in their streets, Tondo is the bitter contrast to the high rises along Roxas Boulevard and the swinging dives of Malate. Even Binondo has rehabilitated its seediness with its well-known restaurants and some of the Philippines' most understated premium addresses. What happened in Tondo nearly 80 years ago forever changed its character, now perpetually dimmed by the battle of Manila's long shadow.

As for the 37th Infantry Division, Beightler could at least stay optimistic about mini-mal casualties and finally getting rid of the Japanese on *his* side of the Pasig river after a week's sparring over territory. Assigning a token unit dubbed the Special Security Force to police the stricken area that had just burned down, the 37th prepared a new series of operations along the Pasig. The objective shifted to Manila's energy infrastructure and this meant the depots on Provisor Island. Meanwhile, as Beightler's HQ moved artillery and supplies to support their upcoming operations, the full strength of the 1st Cavalry Division drove eastward, tracing a broad arc to catch the Japanese by surprise. What hap-pened instead was that the faraway Novaliches dam and San Juan reservoir, along with the Balara Filters beside the University of the Philippines, were taken without too much fuss. In the university campus, however, was a sizeable Japanese garrison occupying the liberal arts and law colleges. Intended as a state-owned academy for professional civil servants, the university's boundaries stretched over untouched meadows and streams, an idyllic setting far removed from Manila's austere Catholic educational institutions dating to the Spanish colonial era.

The fighting over the University of the Philippines probably lasted no more than a day since the main structures on campus, including the Oblation statue at the univer-sity's main entrance, survived with minimal damage after an extensive bombardment by the 1st Cavalry Division's artillery. Capturing the university meant that almost the territory east of Manila was now in American hands. The depth of resistance may have been growing but it became obvious the Japanese fixed positions weren't impregnable as long as concentrated firepower was brought to bear. As the 1st Cavalry Division secured its objectives in record time it slammed into very determined resistance in New Manila. Contrary to its name, this neighbourhood was a small rectangle of land a half hour's drive from Luneta. Its carefully laid-out streets attracted rows of posh dwellings for well-to-do families. Unknown to the approaching Americans, a battalion of Rikusentai had occupied New Manila's houses and 120mm guns were at the ready for menacing any armoured vehicles that might appear. What transpired over a two-day period was an ordeal for the 1st Cavalry Division as 7.7mm and 13mm machine guns and 20mm cannons made any movement on foot impossible. To avoid a stalemate, M4 Shermans of the 44th Tank Battalion accompanied by M7 self-propelled howitzers battered New Manila. The division's towed 105mm and 155mm 'Long Tom' howitzers did their part too and once the division sent its soldiers to clear the ruins, a sizeable inventory of machine guns and abandoned artillery pieces was collected. But, as in Tondo, the Japanese in New Manila had withdrawn to nearby San Juan del Monte under cover of darkness. The amount of ordnance expended was a sure sign that the days ahead weren't going to be easy. Casualties were beginning to mount as well, with dozens of Americans killed and one Sherman tank destroyed by a landmine.

But driving the Japanese out of New Manila did clear the road to Manila proper and on Valentine's Day the 5th and 8th Cavalry regiments, having finished mopping up San Juan del Monte, crossed the Pasig river at two points: at Santa Ana that led straight to Malate just south of Intramuros and at the barren grasslands of San Pedro de Macati. Little by little, the jaws were beginning to close on Iwabuchi's MNDF. Farther south, the 11th Airborne was making serious progress rolling back the defences around Nichols Field, a

The Angels had nothing to compare with the immense Japanese 150mm mortars that rained shells on them.

IJA paratroopers at Clark Field, Luzon. (IJA)

vital installation that could be used to build up forces in Luzon by air. To hasten the 11th's pace, 1st Cavalry Division tank destroyers were sent to assist the paratroopers, whose lightweight 75mm pack howitzers fared poorly against Japanese naval artillery. Seizing Nichols Field also meant access to Fort McKinley and completed the encirclement of the Japanese in Manila.

On the same date that the 1st Cavalry Division laid waste to New Manila, the 37th Infantry Division undertook its own crossings of the Pasig. The first operation involved ferrying troops to the Malacañang Gardens via Landing Ship, Tanks (LSTs) of the 672nd Amphibious Tractor Battalion. The Malacañang Gardens constituted a small park across from Malacañang Palace, an official residence built during the Spanish colonial era for the *Gobernador Heneral*,* and since converted into the Philippines' presidential palace. The importance of Malacañang was symbolic and, luckily for the Americans, the Japanese maintained an insignificant presence in the gardens. Once taken, with minimal losses, the neighbourhood of Paco, just minutes away from Intramuros and Luneta, was within the 37th Infantry Division's grasp.

---

* Governor-General.

But a more important objective lay to the southeast just by the wrecked Quezon bridge whose steel frame, torn by demolition charges, had partially sunk into the Pasig river. For decades, Isla de Provisor or Provisor Island to the Americans, served as a fuel depot and was later converted to a power station. This was both expedient and intentional, for Provisor was an islet on a bend of the Pasig just metres away from another curious islet called the Isla de Convalecencia where a Catholic order had built a small hospice with the Quezon bridge suspended above it. Surrounded by streams that formed a natural moat, the concrete and steel buildings on Provisor housed the generators needed for a bustling city. For Beightler's 37th Infantry Division, taking Provisor meant the power supply for Manila could be preserved and potentially used against the Japanese. This also complemented the 1st Cavalry Division's efforts in securing the metropolitan water utilities. If the operation at Malacañang Gardens was a textbook river crossing the travesty at Provisor was its shameful opposite. In a rare operation launched at daybreak, two companies from the 129th Infantry Regiment attempted to row across the Pasig in flimsy engineer assault boats. When properly used, each of these small craft could fit 15 fully equipped GIs but was light enough for just two men to carry ashore. In yet another instance when the intensity of Japanese resistance proved daunting, a single platoon of G Company had made it ashore but was then pinned down by machine-gun fire. So desperate was their situation that a rescue had to be made at nightfall, still under withering gunfire. To make matters worse, the 129th Infantry were in for a rude surprise that morning when large-diameter rockets began to hit their positions along the Pasig. Although rocket artillery was commonly deployed in Asia and Europe throughout World War II, the Imperial Japanese Army as well as the Imperial Navy were the only militaries that preferred the cumbersome, short-range 200mm and 400mm rockets that were assembled by hand on crude launchers. Much like the utilitarian ease-of-use that went into the 50mm 'knee mortar' that was actually a grenade launcher, the weapon identified as the 'Type 4 20cm rocket launcher' was an unguided munition fired out of a steel tube prepared like a mortar, with a bipod supporting its weight. Without its launcher, an electric fuse and a two-piece wooden 'rail' sufficed as a mechanism for sending off the 20cm or 200mm rocket at least a few kilometres.

Another wave of GIs crossed over to Provisor, only to also get pinned down. With the GIs now trapped on Provisor unable to secure the objective, the full brunt of divisional artillery together with tanks parked along the banks of the Pasig was used against the island. This may have seemed contrary to the 37th Infantry Division's goal of securing the coal-fired power station on Provisor but for the sake of the men trapped on the island and the operational timetable, neutralizing the Japanese on the island as quickly as possible was the next best alternative.

The fight for Provisor lasted three arduous days as persistent shelling reduced the structures on the island. It was simply impossible to send the 129th rowing across the Pasig as they too would have been at the mercy of Japanese machine-gunners who had already either neutralized dozens. Once American casualties were tallied, the deaths at

Provisor reached 25 with several dozen wounded. All the Japanese on the island were assumed killed.

Just as in Tondo, the University of the Philippines and New Manila, the brief, high-intensity battle unravelled in an area still populated by civilians. Once the fighting on Provisor ceased on 10 February, XIV Corps HQ knew beyond any doubt that the battle of Manila was far from over. In the span of a single week entire neighbourhoods had been razed and at least a thousand Japanese killed, with a commensurate humanitarian toll on the population becoming harder to ignore. The Americans also learned how tenacious their foe was. In Leyte, at least, the Japanese army used the local terrain to their advantage and held on for precious weeks amid a deteriorating logistical situation. In Manila the Rikusentai had no geographical advantages but the ample stores of weapons and ammunition taken from the wrecked buildings they fortified showed how determined they were to fight against the odds. The dangers posed by booby traps and mines kept both civilians and Americans on edge, restricting their freedom of movement; this partially explains why a sudden exodus of *Manileños* never happened in early February, apart from the fact the main bridges over the Pasig river were impassable. If residents weren't outright detained inside a school or a church by Japanese soldiers, the numerous roadblocks, fortifications and guard posts around Intramuros prevented escape by car or carriage for families living in Binondo, Ermita and Malate.

But Provisor wasn't exactly a setback. It gave the 37th Infantry Division another foothold on the opposite side of the Pasig and expanded the territory under their control. To chart their progress since the beginning of the month, Beightler's troops had secured a wide area around the University of Santo Tomas, including vital locations such as Malacañang Palace—converted to divisional HQ—and the main business district, leaving the Japanese forces across the river within range of American artillery. If the motivation for a direct assault on Intramuros using small boats and pontoon bridges appeared wanting, there were good reasons why limited encirclement operations took place instead. The dead and wounded from the Provisor operation, as well as the sudden emergence of rockets and other types of artillery directed at the Americans, provoked caution rather than rashness. If XIV Corps HQ directed Beightler to seize Intramuros with utmost haste, casualties would have skyrocketed. This explains why the use of artillery and tanks increased as the month progressed. The Americans needed to eliminate the enemy without feeding a GI meat grinder. Or so XIV Corps HQ thought.

If the 37th Infantry Division succeeded in throwing out the Japanese from the northern half of Manila, the 1st Cavalry Division fulfilled its end on a much grander scale. Since the liberation at Santo Tomas, Mudge's troops had carved out a semi-circle encompassing the eastern portions of Manila and its outskirts. Compared to the ruination of Provisor over three days, the 1st Cavalry secured the vital water infrastructure that fed the city without inflicting significant damage. Although the battles for the University of the Philippines and New Manila afforded them their share of hardship, once two of the 1st Cavalry's brigades crossed the Pasig river at Santa Ana and San Pedro de Macati the division lunged southward to boost the flailing efforts of the 11th Airborne against the

MNDF's Southern Force. What gave the 11th Airborne so much grief were the Japanese 120mm naval gun emplacements around Nichols Field and the heavy mortars that outranged the Angels' own pack howitzers. With the 1st Cavalry Division joining the fray, the 11th Airborne Division subdued Fort McKinley on 17 February, finishing the total encirclement of Manila.

As XIV Corps drew closer to the heart of the city, a single ambiguous episode transpired that spelled immeasurable suffering for the civilians trapped in their homes. When the fighting finally ended the US Army ascertained that radio and written correspondence between Rear Admiral Iwabuchi and the Shimbu Group HQ had

A man and his dog, in a foxhole on a Philippine beach. (US Coast Guard / NARA)

gone uninterrupted for weeks as XIV Corps' hold on Manila's outskirts tightened. It was discovered that Iwabuchi had, in fact, moved his command to Fort McKinley—the same Fort McKinley besieged by the 11th Airborne Division—outside Manila for a brief period but returned just as the 1st Cavalry Division was preparing to cross the Pasig river. Then, on 17 February, he received separate belated orders from Shimbu Group HQ and Yamashita's own HQ in Northern Luzon for an immediate withdrawal from Manila. The former communiqué assured him a counterattack from the east would soon transpire, one that would target the 1st Cavalry Division's flank. Iwabuchi replied that exiting the city was impossible. On that fateful day, the 37th Infantry Division was already in Paco just east of Intramuros and the 1st Cavalry Division had reached Dewey Boulevard that led straight to Luneta and the Manila Hotel. Indeed, after the war, while the battle of Manila was portrayed as a singular tragedy in the greater struggle against Japan's militarist empire, American sources claimed GIs found written orders distributed to Japanese soldiers instructing them to eliminate the city's residents as a contingency against local guerrillas. But none of these incriminating documents can be found today. Appalling civilian casualties are the hallmark of the battle and its most resonant aspect. Did Iwabuchi receive word from his superiors to hold on till the end and take as many civilians down with him?

6. THE GENKO LINE

The difficulties faced by XIV Corps were pedestrian compared to what awaited the 11th Airborne Division when they reached the Route 1 highway and the Parañaque suburbs. Whereas the 1st Cavalry Division had ample room to manoeuvre towards its objectives, the Angels were tasked with seizing Nichols Field on the southernmost outskirts of Manila, and Fort McKinley some two miles to the east. What they didn't count on was that the MNDF's Southern Force had established one of the strangest—and strongest—fortifications encountered anywhere in the Philippines. A network of more than a thousand hardened machine-gun nests supported by large-calibre guns and mortars formed a barrier from the Manila Bay shoreline to Laguna Lake. The Genko Line seemed impregnable when traced on a map, with the Angels unable to concentrate their strength against any single point on the Line. When the Rikusentai blew the bridges over the Pasig river to block XIV Corps, the Angels were barely in Manila's southern outskirts with the 511th Parachute Infantry Regiment leading the way, albeit with no small amount of caution. The resistance they met crossing the Parañaque river finally put a stop to the easy progress they had enjoyed since the Nasugbu landings. The Angels had their first taste of urban combat in Parañaque too. Unable to move forward because of incessant Japanese machine-gun fire, the 511th spent an anxious evening waiting for their artillery support, which, when it came up, battered the opposite shore until daybreak. Rather than press on to their main objective on 5 February, the 511th spent two days extending their reach inside Pasay, the last municipality before entering Manila from the south, and sharpening their street-fighting skills until the reinforced 188th Infantry Regiment took position east of Nichols Field.

The battle for Nichols Field started in earnest on 7 February and, as with other flashpoints around Manila, the firepower levelled at the Americans frustrated their momentum. Defending the Genko Line and Nichols Field were two battalions of Rikusentai designated the Southern Force. At their disposal were 44 large-calibre naval guns taken from ships and emplaced in dugouts, 164 anti-aircraft guns, hundreds of 7.7mm machine guns and, to further deter the enemy, depth charges and sea mines repurposed as booby traps. It deserves repeating the Angels were still part of the Eighth Army led by Eichelberger when the battle for the Genko Line commenced. This arrangement had its own drawbacks. Foremost was the lack of support from Sixth Army and XIV Corps, whose 1st Cavalry Division was drawing nearer to the 11th Airborne as the days went on. The best the Angels could muster, once they arrived from Nasugbu, were the 674th and 675th Field Artillery battalions and their pack howitzers. It helped, even if just a little.

But the 511th Parachute forged ahead. Having reached Liberatd Avenue, the edge of Pasay that formed a boundary with Manila, the 511th turned east to assist the 188th, reinforced

A Japanese Model 96 25mm anti-aircraft gun captured at the Genko Line.

with an additional battalion from the 187th Infantry Regiment, to 'choke' Nichols Field. Both units were quickly mired in the same type of fighting that had frustrated their counterparts in XIV Corps. Unlike the 37th Infantry Division and the 1st Cavalry Division, the Angels had precious few heavy weapons—only light mortars and batteries of 75mm and 105mm pack howitzers suited for close range—and their logistics were precarious. With the rest of the 11th Airborne Division stretched between Parañaque and the Nasugbu beachhead, its flanks were left exposed and vulnerable to attack. It was hard on the wounded too. If they couldn't be treated by a divisional emergency ward close to the front lines, a crude airstrip on Nasugbu was the only way to get them better treatment in Leyte.

Progress from 7 to 9 February was dismal, although the 511th showed their mettle against the Rikusentai. Elsewhere in the Pacific, the Marines saw the Special Naval

The Japanese air defences outside Manila, like this tandem 40mm cannon, were used against infantry.

Landing Forces whom they encountered in their island-hopping battles as Japan's own marines, trained and tested to the same rugged standard as their American counterparts. Yet in and around Manila, when up against the US Army, the Rikusentai wilted in the face of the raw determination shown by their attackers. One explanation for this disparity in performance was the manpower deployed to the MNDF's Southern Force. Rather than hardened veterans, they were green recruits left to fend for themselves. In the first three days of battle for Nichols Field, the 511th's own casualties paled compared to the enemy's in their dugouts and pillboxes. With little more than hand grenades, flamethrowers and decent marksmanship, the Angels managed to cut off Nichols Field and reach Manila proper. Meanwhile, it fell on the reinforced 188th Infantry to seize the main objective, which it attempted on 7 February with a brazen assault on foot. This caused a spike in casualties amid scenes of uncommon valour. By 10 February, however, the desperate need for artillery support saw the transfer of the 11th Airborne Division from the Eight Army to the Sixth Army. The combined strength of air and artillery support in the following days allowed the 188th, with help from the 511th, to capture Nichols Field on 13 February. The victory was pyrrhic, much like at Provisor Island to the north, since the damage done on the air base was so extensive that it was judged unfit for use, although a company of paratroopers from the 511th did manage to take off from it on 23 February to rescue civilian PoWs in Los Baños to the south.

Still, the leftover booby traps, landmines and unexploded ordnance kept the entire facility from thorough rehabilitation. Another curious find at Nichols Field, in a scenario that was earlier observed at Clark Field in Central Luzon, was the scattering of equipment and ordnance. The Angels found aircraft and engines partially hidden under trees on roadsides and street corners, in poor attempts at camouflage. After three years, it seemed, the Japanese had done little to improve Nichols Field other than erect fortifications over a wide area. Japanese military aviation in the Philippines was a foregone conclusion at that stage in the war, anyway, with the biggest threat coming from *kamikazes* disrupting shipping. The source of the Angels' troubles was also found on the Nichols Field perimeter: large-calibre naval guns emplaced in dugouts and set at ground level. The most menacing of these was the Model 3 12cm or 120mm naval gun, a type favoured by the Rikusentai, whose obsolescence as a large-calibre anti-aircraft weapon lent itself well to redeployment as artillery, surpassing the American M101 105mm howitzer's range. Attached to a pivoting mount that was bolted to a ship's deck, when transferred to dry land the Model 3 was accurate enough for use as an anti-tank weapon. At Nichols Field, however, it was responsible for delaying the 188th's progress for at least two days. An additional threat were the Model 96 two- and three-barrelled 25mm anti-aircraft guns. The largest variant was armed with three guns arranged in a row, or what is known as a triple-fixed mount and fed by large box magazines loaded from above the receiver. Unlike the 120mm guns, the Type 96s were not originally intended for on-board use but were the Japanese navy's preferred short- to medium-range defence artillery for airstrips and other sensitive locations. The 10° depression of the Type 96's barrel meant it could be used against land targets as well. At Nichols Field the Type 96 joined the 7.7mm and 13mm machine guns to form a veritable ring of lead to stop the Americans. Capable of blowing soft-skinned vehicles to smithereens from a thousand metres, it was fortunate the Angels fought on foot as proper airborne units should.

Still another headache were the dual mounted 40mm anti-aircraft guns based on a Vickers design. These might have seemed strange additions to the MNDF's arsenal but weapons copied from British and other European designs were common in the Japanese navy. This had much to do with expedience as with heritage. As far back as the late 19th century, when Japan was still assembling and modernizing its fleet, British advisers, methods and ships formed the institution's main capabilities. It was no coincidence that the guns on many Japanese warships, like the dreaded 120mm, were copied from old British artillery pieces. This relationship carried on for decades until, with utmost irony, Japan went to war against the Allies. Many of the large-calibre weapons deployed by the Japanese in the Pacific were often decades old—obsolescent yet lethal against unprotected infantry.

An absolute terror for the Angels at Nichols Field, as well as Allied troops everywhere in the Pacific, were the Model 93 150mm mortars. With an explosive charge greater than the 107mm heavy mortars of the US Army, the Model 93s were a menace on the battlefield and an unspecified number were deployed at the Genko Line. Designed to be carried in separate parts and assembled for action, the Model 93 still required several operators and had a limited range that extended to just 2,000 metres. Truly unfortunate for the Angels was to come under fire from 90mm anti-aircraft guns. Unlike the 120mm and 37mm pieces, these were not Japanese and, based on accounts of the fighting at Nichols Field, the US Army's long-range M1 anti-aircraft artillery was now being used against American forces. The M1 was produced in the late 1930s and entered service in 1941. It seems that the original defences at Nichols Field at the time of Homma's Luzon invasion had been preserved and it was these pieces that bedevilled the Angels with lethal airbursts above their huddled forms.

Aside from enemy weaponry, the Angels had to eliminate countless fortifications stretching from Parañaque to the waters of Laguna. These usually came in three types. The most common was an earthen bunker that resembled a molehill with enough room for at least a 7.7mm machine gun. Whoever laid these out at Fort McKinley miscalculated their arrangement as the Angels managed to flank them with ease and eliminate their occupants from the rear. Another tactic was to fire a white phosphorus round from a howitzer to spot it for an incoming airstrike. Unlike XIV Corps in Manila, the 11th Airborne Division had the advantage of having Air Corps radio operators embedded with them. Fighters and dive-bombers from as far away as Lingayen would aid the Angels in their two-week operation, with equally dependable and spectacular results.

Another type of earthen bunker were the ones built with such engineering talent as to almost conceal the structure from sight. These were indistinguishable from the local terrain and, when located near vegetation, forced the Americans to carefully plan their movements before swarming the Japanese machine-gunners holding them off. Like in Manila, however, the Angels never encountered sharpshooters or any scoped firearms.

A more difficult obstruction were the reinforced concrete bunkers that surrounded Nichols Field. Some were large enough to serve as gun emplacements and proved difficult to eliminate. The 11th Airborne's own records include numerous photographs of these structures, some of which resembled mausoleums rising from the ground. With their walls packed tight with heaps of soil, direct fire from howitzers proved useless and the best recourse was getting close enough for a GI with an M2 flamethrower to bathe its interior with burning gasoline.

A truly baffling find for the Angels at Nichols Field was an underground command post that was at least two floors deep. Examined after the fighting, the structure was large enough for at least a platoon to hide in. Although a far cry from the concrete and steel air raid shelters under Fort McKinley that were built during the Commonwealth, the secret 'house' at Nichols Field never revealed its true purpose: was it reserved for VIPs or a clandestine war room?

By 19 February, the 11th Airborne Division had subsumed the Genko Line and linked up with the 1st Cavalry Division. Almost the entirety of Manila, save for Intramuros and its nearby buildings, was under XIV Corps control. Although outgunned, the Angels had annihilated the MNDF's Southern Force and killed more than 5,000 Japanese troops in 16 days of non-stop fighting.

But there was one last important job for the division. Since the beginning of the month plans had been afoot to capture the Los Baños concentration camp located southeast of

Soldiers belonging to the 11th Airborne watch over a baby after the raid on Los Baños.

Laguna Lake. Once again, the tireless 511th Parachute Infantry Regiment was tasked with the mission. But instead of redeploying the entire unit, only the 1st Battalion was assigned to the Los Baños mission with assistance from the 6th Ranger Battalion and Filipino guerrillas acting as scouts. The rescue operation was an elaborate one involving B Company of 1st Battalion dropping near the objective and a secondary force, the rest of the 1st Battalion, arriving from Laguna Lake by amphibious tractor. D-Day was in the morning of 23 February, the same date as XIV Corps' furious bombardment of Intramuros. Once on the ground, B Company eliminated the camp guards and rescued 2,147 civilians who were then transported to safety. The flawless Los Baños rescue was the last significant mission of the daring and dogged 11th Airborne in Luzon and several months later the Angels became the first American unit assigned to occupy Japan.

After the war, every trace of the Genko Line and the Japanese military's brief sojourn at Nichols Field and Fort McKinley disappeared. Gone are the bombs and the pillboxes that menaced the 11th Airborne Division that February.

There was also a maddening twist at the end of their struggle. On 17 February, elements of the Shimbu Group struck at the 1st Cavalry Division's flanks from the Sierra Madre

B-24s of the Fifth Air Force dispersed at Clark Field, 1945. (San Diego Air & Space Museum)

mountains but were repelled. It was later reported an estimated 1,900 Japanese troops had vanished like phantoms from McKinley. They had escaped, it was assumed, under orders from Shimbu Group HQ. Besides, the Japanese did have a talent for manoeuvring undetected. The combat records aren't too clear about the significance of this minor retreat. Did it hasten the liberation of Manila by sparing the Angels from another day or two of combat? The disappearance of the Japanese at McKinley did support raw intelligence that claimed the Shimbu Group HQ tried facilitating an orderly withdrawal of troops from Manila, but only the survivors at Fort McKinley complied since Iwabuchi was trapped in the city with what was left of his Rikusentai.

Nichols Field assumed a new role as Manila's reconstruction and ensuing sprawl made it immensely valuable to the Philippine state. Today, the area that used to be Nichols Field is the Villamor airbase, the headquarters of the Philippine Air Force named after a daring Filipino-American pilot Jesús Villamor who shot down two Japanese planes over Luzon in 1941 before joining MacArthur in Australia. The airbase is now wedged between a sprawling luxury hotel and casino and the immense Ninoy Aquino International Airport whence thousands of Filipinos leave the country each day to work abroad and support their families back home. Parañaque itself is no longer just a half-empty plain with a small coastal town but an overcrowded city of 700,000 people. Bowing to the pressures of urbanization, Fort McKinley has disappeared under a blanket of real-estate development and the very ground trodden by the Angels as they rolled back the Genko Line is now the *Libingan Ng Mga Bayani* or the Hero's Cemetery, the final resting place of Filipino soldiers and statesmen. A short drive away is the Manila American Cemetery laid out in concentric circles for the 17,184 graves of American servicemen who perished in the Southwest Pacific. The pristine address surrounded by office towers and suburbs is one of the more remarkable memorials to World War II in Asia, its white gravestones occupying an untouched parcel of land shared with the Philippine Army's Fort Andres Bonifacio, whose namesake—his statue, rather—greeted the 1st Cavalry Division's thrilling entrance at Grace Park, Caloocan, on their way to save the hopeful prisoners at Santo Tomas.

Hurrah for the Douglas SBD-5 Dauntless

It is a well-established fact that MacArthur's SWPA HQ forbade airstrikes on Manila despite the frequent requests of the XIV Corps commanders, who resorted to concentrated artillery barrages instead. But air support did play a role on the outskirts of the city. As the 11th Airborne Division surrounded Nichols Field, bombers from as far away as Mindoro—a large island off Batangas to the south—and Lingayen flew multiple sorties against the occupied airfield. The most common type for these missions was the Douglas SBD-5 Dauntless of the US Marine Corps' MAG-12 squadron.

Dauntless divebombers.

Though withdrawn from service in the US Navy in mid-1944, the USMC flew the last batches of the Dauntless to provide close air support for the SWPA. The Dauntless, also known as the A-24, was an icon of the key battles in the Pacific theatre. Since the initial batch of more than a hundred SBDs rolled off the Douglas Aircraft Company's production line in 1939, the US Navy's urgent need for carrier-based dive-bombers swelled orders. Douglas Aircraft's own tally reached 5,936 A-24s built in its factories by the end of the war. The SBDs proved their worth in countless engagements, including Midway.

The Marine squadron known as MAG-12 flew the last SBD-5s over Luzon in the early months of 1945. While the 1st Cavalry Division raced to Manila in February, their hasty progress was ensured by a protective umbrella of SBD-5s overhead. Japanese fighters were scarce by that time, with nearly 2,000 destroyed since the Leyte invasion. This meant the SBD-5 gunners, ensconced in turrets armed with twin .30-calibre machine guns, had little to worry about. As the 11th Airborne slowly dismantled the Genko Line and helped complete the encirclement of Manila, the SBD-5s maintained a busy schedule obliterating the Japanese defenders. But the dive-bombers never flew sorties over Manila proper and, luckily for the pilots, no MAG-12 aircraft were lost to enemy fire.

7. BLOODY HELL

The two weeks of combat between XIV Corps and Iwabuchi's MNDF left no respite for Manila's helpless population. The Americans were already aware of the cruel treatment inflicted by the Japanese on their prisoners, apparent from the state of the civilians they rescued at Santo Tomas and Bilibid. But what of the average *Manileños*? How did they cope?

With the city locked down for months, the majority of the residents were trapped in their homes. The creeping helplessness became unbearable as the fighting erupted across the Pasig river while the fires from Tondo cast a dark shadow over Manila. The worst was yet to come for the Filipinos who had survived three years of Japanese tyranny. For one family, the Quirinos of Ermita, the distant rumble of shellfire was terrifying. The family patriarch, Elpidio Quirino, feared for the well-being of his wife and their five children. A Commonwealth-era politician who refused to join the puppet government on principle, like many among Manila's political class, he and his family lived in a state of semi-permanent house arrest, always fearing the summons from the invaders. With the thrill of learning of the American landings at Leyte the previous year a distant memory, the Quirino household did their best to wait out the war, or so they thought. As XIV Corps artillery duelled with the MNDF's own emplacements during the battle for Provisor Island, on 9 February the Quirino's sense of dread turned to panic when a stray shell set their home ablaze.

Taking the children and whatever valuables they could muster, the Quirinos quit their doomed residence on Colorado Street to seek refuge with their in-laws just minutes away. Quirino sent his eldest son Tomas ahead while his wife looked after their two youngest daughters. Once they were out on the street a nearby guard post opened fire and mowed down the whole family. Elpidio Quirino himself was unscathed and both his eldest son Tomas and eldest daughter Victoria pulled through with minor injuries. The casualties were his wife, Alicia Syquia-Quirino, her infant daughter Fe and the youngest daughter Norma. Armando Quirino, the youngest son tasked with holding the family's valuables, tried saving his mother but was shot in the head. Rather than live the rest of his days a broken man, Quirino survived the war and returned to politics, serving as vice-president in President Manuel Roxas's brief administration once the Philippines gained its independence. President Quirino's own term lasted from 1948 until 1953, a period when he sought to normalize ties with Japan and build a viable post-war national economy.

The horror of the Quirino family's demise wasn't an accident and there are enough records from the battle chronicling Japanese excess. In what first seemed like a ruthless disregard for civilian lives, once it was apparent the Americans were approaching Intramuros, the pattern of violence spread to every neighbourhood still held by the

Rikusentai. It simply cannot be argued that the XIV Corps artillery inflicted a collateral death toll on Manila so great that the Americans deserve equal blame for the battle's grim outcome. On the contrary, there are sufficient accounts from survivors revealing how the Japanese turned on the civilian population of Manila from the second week of February until month's end. A decision was made in what was left of Iwabuchi's crumbling HQ to target both Filipinos and foreigners living in Manila and generous leeway was given for the *methods* used, thereby justifying the rape and ritualized murder—bayoneting, decapitation, immolation and death-by-grenade—that happened on a vast scale. No serious appraisal of Manila in 1945 can be read without dwelling on the humanitarian disaster of the events of February and March. What follows are brief portraits of Japanese brutality visited on unarmed civilians for inexplicable reasons, gleaned from an old document containing survivors' testimonies published by XIV Corps in April 1945. The lesson for the reader is to show that the battle of Manila wasn't just a tactical confrontation pitting a Western military against an Asian military, but a hideous example of indiscriminate force used on a captive population in wartime. Each of these instances will be contrasted by the military events that occurred on the same date.

Recalling the murder of the Quirinos, an even worse fate descended on the Maldonados. Like so many other families in Manila, Mr. and Mrs. Maldonado fled their house when it caught fire after getting hit by a rocket. The young couple sought shelter in the residence of a doctor and were joined by their relatives and neighbours. The house was later attacked by at least a platoon of Japanese soldiers, who crammed the men inside the bathroom and the women in the kitchen. Fearing rape, some of the women tried to flee but were mercilessly beaten and shot. Mrs. Maldonado herself was stabbed with a bayonet and her sister murdered in front of her. The Japanese then threw grenades inside the bathroom. Mr. Maldonado managed to kick one away, at the expense of mangling his foot when it detonated, but additional bombs killed almost everyone else, including Mrs. Maldonado's father. At least a dozen other refugees perished when the house burned down. Mrs. Maldonado's version of events indicates she and her husband fled on 17 February, while Manila was completely encircled and the 1st Cavalry Division had cleared every major landmark south of Luneta, and the 37th Infantry was firmly in control of the Pasig river. This atrocity took place in either Ermita or Paco, two neighbourhoods where a frightening number of massacres took place. The methodology of the Japanese is also telling as they segregated their hostages before attempting to rape the women and kill the men all at once: gender segregation was always the initial activity in mass-murdering Filipinos in Manila, the true scale of which the Americans witnessed when they attacked Intramuros on 23 February.

The most sordid and utterly gut-wrenching episode in the battle took place at the Bayview Hotel, a landmark on the corner of Dewey Boulevard and Luneta. On 9 February the fighting on Provisor Island compelled the residents of Ermita to vacate their homes but they were arrested by the Japanese instead. Ermita, of course, was a well-to-do neighbourhood but this didn't spare its women from a nightmarish ordeal perpetrated by the Japanese. Once the refugees were collected at Plaza Ferguson, Japanese soldiers began conducting a familiar routine: the men and women were segregated. The effort turned sinister once the women were arranged by age and appearance. Those with the fairest complexions, ranging from their early teens to middle age, were imprisoned at the Bayview Hotel, which was crowded with Japanese troops. Their fate was clear: the hotel had been converted into a whorehouse. Kept in the ballrooms on the lower floors and nourished with a meagre diet of water and biscuits, the women were dragged away helpless to satiate the Bayview's eager patrons. Brought alone or in groups to a room and stripped naked, long lines of Japanese soldiers took turns raping them. Once finished, the dishevelled victims were returned to their holding pen where some unfortunate mothers tried consoling their violated teenage daughters. The cycle of rapes continued for almost a full week until the Bayview Hotel got hit by artillery. Survivors of this impromptu 'rape camp' recalled wandering dazed as the city burned around them, their families nowhere to be found. In a cruel twist the women who survived Bayview were fortunate. Other Filipinas raped by the Japanese were either bayoneted to death once their attacker had finished with them or shot if they resisted. A particular female survivor from the Bayview contracted venereal disease after she and her sister were raped multiple times one night. Her personal testimony stands out as the most detailed yet regarding organized rape of civilian women during the struggle for Manila.

According to Esther Garcia Moras, she and 25 other women of various ages were locked in a room at the Bayview Hotel and plied with drinks. Her 14-year-old sister Evangeline was spared from being raped because of her period. But Esther's other sister wasn't as lucky. Neither was she. "The Japanese soldiers would come in with candies and choose the girl they wanted," she recalled. "After taking my sister, one Japanese returned and took me to a room and locked the door. He pushed me to the floor and did it—it hurt me." As if the ordeal wasn't bad enough, as soon as her violator finished, more arrived to take their turn. "About twelve or fifteen ones took me," Esther told the XIV Corps investigators. "The last one was so large that he hurt me, I actually bled. He took all of my clothes and put me on the bed. He kept me there for half an hour, raping me several times."

Based on Esther's testimony, she and her sisters were trapped in the Bayview Hotel for three days without any provisions. But after her initial ordeal at the hands of so many Japanese soldiers, the violations stopped. Let go when the hotel caught fire, the sisters vainly sought help. Esther's sister was still bleeding from injuries to her sex organs after four Japanese took turns raping her.

As if their situation couldn't have got any worse, their mother Mrs. Garcia was later imprisoned in the hotel too but was spared because of her age. She endured the trauma of consoling her daughters Esther and Priscilla after they had been violated by the soldiers. Adding to the family's miseries, as the Garcias fled down Arquiza Street on or before Valentine's Day, Esther's 11-year-old brother Joaquin died from blood loss after his leg had been sliced off by shrapnel from a bomb blast. If these glimpses of horror reveal anything, it's the sublime cruelty the Japanese were more than willing to visit on innocent people.

The rise and fall of the Rikusentai rape camp on Dewey Boulevard fitted a crucial timeline, however. The night the fair women of Ermita were taken hostage was when

Beightler's 37th Infantry Division launched their tenuous trips across the Pasig river. Once the Bayview was evacuated, the 1st Cavalry Division finished its long drive around Manila and the 5th and 12th Cavalry regiments crossed the Pasig at Santa Ana and Macati. Meanwhile, the 11th Airborne had taken Nichols Field and Pierson Task Force was about to strike east of Fort McKinley with tanks and air support. Indeed, the suffering of *Manileños* was an upsetting contrast to the tactical successes less than an hour's drive from their torment. Whatever remained of Iwabuchi's MNDF and Rikusentai were trapped in several addresses and these were soon eliminated by the 1st Cavalry's squadrons. Racing from Santa Ana down to Vito Cruz, between 15 and 16 February, the De La Salle College, the Rizal Stadium and the Manila Yacht Club were cleared of Japanese stragglers.

A bizarre fight broke out inside the Rizal Stadium, a sports complex with a baseball field with a seating capacity for thousands, when the defenders had to be machine-gunned at close range because they were so well concealed in sandbagged hideouts underneath the bleachers. The Rizal Stadium was an unapologetically American edifice transplanted to the other side of the Pacific. As if the colonial amenities around Manila weren't enough to tickle the sensibilities of a large American expatriate population, the Rizal Stadium was built with Olympic grandeur in mind and when it opened in 1934 it was possible for 10,000 spectators to enjoy either a baseball or football game. The Japanese occupation had little use for the venue but machine guns were emplaced anyway to meet the Americans. On 16 February, the 1st Cavalry troops who stormed the stadium called in three Sherman tanks to clear the baseball field. Over two hours and unknown quantities of machine-gun ammunition and high-explosive rounds later, the Japanese were eliminated by late afternoon. Of course, at this point in the battle the Americans understood that operational tempo was paramount. To expedite the total encirclement of Manila, 1st Cavalry Division HQ transferred the 1st Cavalry Brigade to the 37th Infantry Division. This was so Beightler, from his command post across the Pasig, could direct it to seize a huge swathe of urban terrain stretching from Dewey Boulevard to Taft Avenue. The objective covered a vast residential district and allowed the 37th's troops to reconnoitre Manila City Hall, another splendid Commonwealth structure, just across the street from Intramuros.

In mere days the last complete unit of Iwabuchi's MNDF, the 2nd Naval Battalion, was eliminated, the 1st Cavalry Division counting 750 enemy killed compared to their own 40 KIA. On 20 February, before the final apocalyptic push into the walled city, the 37th Infantry Division's 129th and 145th Infantry regiments crossed from Ermita and, with support from Shermans and M7 Priests, blasted their way to Manila City Hall. It looked as if the fighting would soon be over but XIV Corps HQ was fully aware that thousands of the enemy were determined to make a last stand at Intramuros. Yet until the end of the month, the civilian toll these pitched battles wrought was never determined, the scale of the genocide simply unimaginable. For the past three years the US Army in the Southwest Pacific had never had to deal with a humanitarian crisis as it slogged between islands and steaming jungles. In Manila, however, as long as the American GIs battled from street to building to landmark, Japanese soldiers were murdering and raping at a frenzied pace. Such was the hideous game unravelling in the woebegone corners of a doomed metropolis. Liberating the capital of the Philippines through methodical destruction occurred at the same time an occupying army was doing its best to murder the residents with utmost efficiency.

As carnage engulfed Manila, the shock of one loyal *Manileño* had a lasting impact on Philippine history. MacArthur had spent his entire adult life in the Philippines and called Manila home. His own father had led American troops in Manila at the turn of the century and he, the son, had the rare distinction of being made a field marshal by the late President Quezon. "In this city," he reminisced, "my mother had died, my wife had been courted, my son had been born."

With Yamashita's divisions crumbling throughout Luzon, MacArthur made it a habit to check on the progress of XIV Corps as they battled for the city day after day and even watched from a distance as a combined air and sea assault by XI Corps retook Corregidor, the lonesome island fortress guarding Manila Bay, on 16 February. When he inspected the island after the successful operation, MacArthur was shown the tunnel where the last thousand Japanese defenders blew themselves up in an horrific mass suicide.

The commander of the SWPA later joined the 37th Infantry Division as it encircled Intramuros. MacArthur fails to give a date in his memoir published before died, but the description of the event suggests late February, just before the climactic assault on Iwabuchi's final stronghold. "I was anxious to rescue as much as I could of my home atop the Manila Hotel and accompanied a leading patrol of the [37th Infantry] division," he wrote. "We reached the New Luneta, but were temporarily pinned down on Burnham Green by machine gun fire from the hotel itself. Suddenly, the penthouse blazed into flame. They [Japanese] had fired it. I watched, with indescribable feelings, the destruction of my fine military library, my souvenirs, my personal belongings of a lifetime."

If MacArthur's account seemed tactless in the context of the innocent people being killed across the city, this stems from his own reservations than a disregard for human dignity. Combat records from after the battle reveal that the 1st Squadron of the 12th Cavalry Regiment (1st Cavalry Division) was responsible for taking back the Manila Hotel on 21 February. The location had been shelled the day before while troops had dug in at Burnham Green, a small park south of the hotel lobby, to block any attempted escape. If MacArthur had indeed witnessed the destruction of his former residence, it is possible he arrived under escort as 1st Squadron cleared its topmost floors. By his own retelling, a furious MacArthur entered the battered structure to see what was left of the ruined penthouse suite he used to call home. He found a dead Japanese colonel by the entrance where he had kept two ornamental jars gifted by the Emperor of Japan. When a lieutenant quipped, "Nice going, chief," to the CO of the SWPA, MacArthur could barely contain his rage: "But there was nothing nice about it to me," he wrote in his memoir. "I was tasting the last acid dregs [of] the bitterness of a devastated and beloved home."

On 27 February, just 20 days after MacArthur's own staff let it slip that Manila had been 'liberated' and in the same tense week when the last Japanese holdouts were being wiped out around Luneta by howitzers at close-range, the commander of the SWPA arrived at Malacañang Palace for a minor occasion. Spared from the apocalyptic scenes just across the Pasig river, Malacañang hosted the newly arrived government-in-exile led by President Sergio Osmeña. On that day, MacArthur's job was restoring 'full constitutional government' to the Philippine Commonwealth with a prepared speech. But the flamboyant commander found the moment, in his own words, "soul-wrenching".

On the drive to Malacañang earlier in the day, with distant gunfire still audible, MacArthur saw up close the aftermath of what XIV Corps' tenacity and the Rikusentai's stubbornness had produced: "As I passed through the streets with their burned-out piles of rubble, the air still filled with the stench of decaying unburied dead, the tall and stately trees that had been the mark of a gracious city were nothing but ugly scrubs pointing broken fingers at the sky," MacArthur wrote. "Once famous buildings were now shells. The street signs and familiar landmarks were gone. One moved by sense of direction rather than sight."

When delivering his remarks to President Osmeña, MacArthur suddenly choked on his words and fell silent rather than let his emotions overcome him. "My voice broke, I could not go on," he recalled. What is unmentioned in MacArthur's telling and completely absent from documents dating to the battle of Manila is he may have been momentarily immersed in what the GIs and shell-shocked residents had to put up with on the streets: not just debris and wreckage, but rotting corpses everywhere, many of them women and children.

Decades after the battle, MacArthur's recollections from 1945 might have glossed over the sickening horror he witnessed on that fateful visit to Malacañang. Rather than dwell on the memory, he confessed his emotional state. "It seemed only the culmination of a panorama of physical and spiritual disaster," he wrote of liberated Manila. "It had killed something inside me to see my men die."

The Old Hospital (Engineering Building) of Santo Tomas University, 1945. Around it are shanties built by Allied PoWS and internees in the Japanese Santo Tomas Internment Centre. (US Army)

Above: 421st Night Fighter Squadron Northrop P-61B-20-NO Black Widow 43-8317 landing at Puetro Princesa Airfield, Tacloban, Leyte, 8 February 1945. (USAF / USGOV-PD)

Below: The Manila Port Area, 1945.

Above: The Agricultural Building, battered and pockmarked.

Below: The Jones Bridge and the Colegio de San Juan de Letran in ruins.

Above: Douglas MacArthur inspects the ruined Manila hotel, February 1945.

Below: American troops cross the Pasig river.

Above: American soldiers in front of the Manila Post Office, February 1945. (John Tewell)

Below: A GI searching for the elusive enemy, Intramuros. (John Tewell)

Above: American
soldiers take cover
behind jeeps and tanks
on Dewey Boulevard,
Manila, February 1945.
(John Tewell)

Right: A soldier
walking along the
obliterated Solano
Street inside
the Walled City
of Intramuros,
March 1945.
(John Tewell)

Above: American tanks fire on the Legislature Building from Manila City Hall, February 1945. (John Tewell)

Below: Filipino children in the rubble of Manila.

Above: GIs on Avenida Rizal, Manila, February 1945. (John Tewell)

Below: A Sherman tank rumbles down Avenida Rizal.

Above: Manila burns. Seen here is the Post Office Building and the destroyed Santa Cruz bridge.

Left: Six high-ranking Japanese generals and admirals who surrendered at Cebu, shortly after their incarceration in New Bilibid near Manila. One of them reads a copy of Yank magazine. From left: Lt. Gen. Shinpel Fukuei, Maj. Gen. Takeo Manjome, Rear-Adm. Kaku Harada, Maj. Gen. Tadasn Kataoka, Maj. Gen. Isamu Hirai and Maj. Gen. Masuo Yoshiki. (S/Sgt Potter / War Dept / NARA)

8. INTRAMUROS

By late February everything north and west of the Pasig river was now in American hands. But the MNDF still controlled the walled city with untold numbers of hostages trapped inside. A hasty assault would have spelled disaster for the 37th Infantry Division so 155mm and 240mm howitzers were redeployed along the river's edge. Two days of intermittent shelling produced two vital gaps in the stout walls of Intramuros. On the morning of 23 February four battalions of 105mm howitzers, three battalions of 155mm howitzers, a single battery of 240mm howitzers and a token battery of 107mm mortars unleashed hell on the Japanese. The bombardment lasted a full hour, from 0730 until 0830 and was accompanied by salvos from the Shermans and the Hellcats. It was imperative that the volume of high-explosive and armour-piercing rounds (from the tanks) softened up the buildings behind the walls and left them vacant. There were also flamethrower tanks at hand for when the combat got too intense.

Companies of the 129th Infantry crossed the Pasig on flimsy assault boats that delivered them to the southwest bank near Fort Santiago where they entered the breach near the Government Mint and stormed the old citadel from behind. The 145th Infantry took the southeastern route, their objective being the 'Aquarium' at the far end of Intramuros facing Luneta. It must be understood, contrary to what some American historians claim, that Intramuros was neither an ancient nor a medieval fortress but a remarkable example of late 18th-century fortification that the Spanish did their best to maintain until they lost the Philippines in 1898. Seen from above, each of the corners on the Intramuros's continuous walls were shaped like chevrons to give muzzle-loading cannon a wide field of fire. The battlements were far from obsolescent in 1945 and two soldiers on a machine gun could lie crouched for hours, waiting to mow down oncoming attackers. Their relative concealment and the sheer thickness of the concrete around them made return fire useless. For this reason, an impenetrable smokescreen that included bursts of white phosphorus launched from the howitzer batteries concealed the 129th's and 145th's river crossing. Upon reaching the opposite bank the men hurried past the abandoned Post Office that stood between the wrecked Quezon and Santa Cruz bridges.

The 129th's advance was led by L Company and once inside the walled city, movement became precarious. The colonial edifices like the Letran University were bristling with machine-gun nests and to the Americans' surprise, Filipino civilians were still fleeing from their Japanese captors. The situation became even more complicated once they reached Fort Santiago's entrance adorned with the crest of St. James the Moor-killer (*Matamoros*). How the Americans managed to blow a hole through the old stone walls large enough for an M3 Sherman tank remains perplexing, but soldiers from L Company did enter the fort and annihilated the remaining defenders during the course of the night,

Liberated American PoWs were repatriated to the United States as soon as possible.

with some 400 Japanese corpses evident in the morning. It was in the dungeons below the fort where the latest atrocities were discovered: bodies piled on top of each other, all local men. It was ascertained the multitude had been crammed into cells and slaughtered with bayonet and gunshot. This was an horrific bookend to the purges of late 1944, when anyone suspected of aiding the guerrillas was brutalized at the fort.

On 24 February the 145th did their best to protect an estimated 3,000 hostages, this time women and children, who had sought shelter at the San Agustin and Del Monico churches. The timing of the Americans' arrival couldn't have been more fortunate as bodies were again discovered in the bomb shelters underneath the Palacio del Gobernador just across the street from San Agustin. This fitted a pattern where the Japanese used places of worship and other sensitive locations, such as schools and hospitals, to herd civilians into and kill them with cold-blooded efficiency. Evacuating the Intramuros survivors by truck arriving from Pasay, now occupied by the 1st Cavalry Division, proved difficult as the unprotected convoy was at the mercy of Japanese machine-gunners in nearby buildings. When motor transport was too hazardous, the women and children were escorted to the river's edge and taken aboard *bancas* tasked with depositing them in

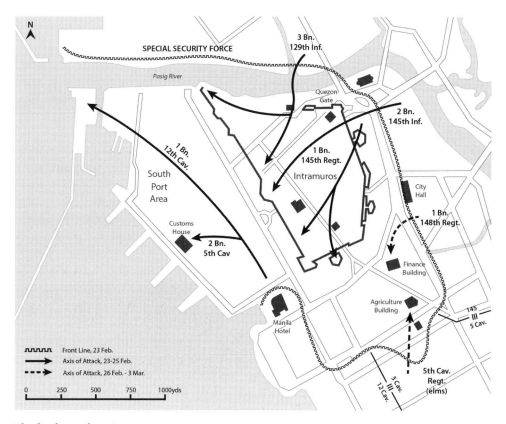

The final assault on Intramuros.

the ruins of Binondo. A pontoon bridge was later assembled to allow the elderly and the wounded to cross on foot. But resistance in the walled city had ebbed at this point and the South Port Area, along with the Manila Hotel that had to be cleared floor by floor, was consolidated on the same day with help from squadrons of the 1st Cavalry Division's 5th and 12th Cavalry regiments. It was during this minor breakthrough when the strangest 'battle' in the vicinity of Intramuros unfolded. After days spent clearing the Manila Hotel room by room, the South Port Area was overrun with relative ease as its defenders capitulated at the sight of Americans. They weren't Japanese, it turned out, but Chinese and Korean dockworkers hastily armed and left to fend for themselves. The South Port Area was soon cleared and army engineers took over. The importance of the port was for supplies to arrive as soon as possible. These would hasten operations in the rest of Luzon and restore the Philippines as a staging area for an assault on the Japanese mainland in the near future.

Yet victory was far from certain. Hundreds of Rikusentai still controlled the administrative buildings outside Intramuros. As for their commander, Iwabuchi, there was no trace of his presence anywhere inside the walled city. The soldiers of the 37th Infantry

Division never found a bunker or enclosure that served as a command post among the gutted buildings. It was later presumed Iwabuchi perished during the initial bombardment on the morning of 23 February. In the two days since the successful assault on Intramuros had commenced, the Americans were burdened with clearing the last pocket of resistance in Manila. The job proved more difficult than anyone expected as nothing less than raw firepower would dislodge the enemy.

Of course, it was terribly ironic for the XIV Corps' battle-weary divisions to wreck the very edifices designed by well-meaning Americans and built for a would-be independent Filipino republic. Laid out with impeccable taste outside the brooding Intramuros, the vital structures of which dated to the military-religious sensibilities of a bygone Spanish empire, the American colonial regime envisioned an inviting cityscape that embodied representative democracy. The urban planner Daniel Burnham was originally commissioned to lay out a series of structures as offices whence the Philippines could be governed. The result, done with the help of his assistant, William E. Parsons, was utterly charming. The Luneta facing Manila Bay was extended to the shoreline, a *New* Luneta, and the slice of land between it and the Rizal Monument was renamed Burnham Green. The Rizal Monument itself was a magnificent tribute to the national hero, Dr. José Protacio Rizal,* done with almost no input from Filipinos. In 1912 an obelisk was erected in Rizal's honour and below it, standing tall on a pedestal, was a statue of the hero by the Swiss sculptor Richard Kissling. For added gravitas, the national hero's remains were interred in the same location.

Behind the Rizal Monument was the breathtaking Wallace Field that stretched to Taft Avenue. Along Taft were the defunct Commonwealth's three main governing structures: the Legislative Building, the Finance Building, and a little farther from both, the Agriculture Building, each embodying the prevailing architectural trends of the era. The Legislative Building's twin courtyards and ostentatious Corinthian columns were unapologetically neoclassical. The best efforts of the US-educated Filipino architect Juan Arellano—whose previous work on the nearby Manila Post Office and Metropolitan Theatre were fine examples of Art Deco—added little to the Legislative Building's evocative severity in concrete. The same qualities applied to the smaller structures of the Agriculture and Finance buildings.

To the northeast of these was Manila City Hall and its iconic clock tower and then south from Taft Avenue was Malate, a respectable neighbourhood that had since been blighted by the fighting. For Manila to be won, the entire complex of tree-lined avenues and grandiose buildings in and around Luneta was consigned to oblivion. Although electricity and water infrastructure were now back in American hands, the most recent intelligence suggested the Japanese had ample stocks of food and munitions in their last-ditch impregnable hideouts.

The Legislative Building was the first to be pummelled. The combined strength of the 37th Infantry Division, augmented by squadrons from the 5th and 12th Cavalry regiments,

---

* Rizal was a Filipino nationalist and revolutionary executed by Spanish firing squad in 1896.

weren't enough to simply rush the objective and secure it. The 44th Tank Battalion's M3 Shermans were deployed at the safest possible distance and, in unison with the 76mm guns of the M18 tank destroyers, rained armour-piercing and high-explosive rounds on the structure. Except for lulls as the evening arrived, the bombardment continued until the next day with assistance from 155mm howitzers and 107mm mortars. The Legislative Building was finally taken on 26 February after American soldiers flushed the last stragglers out with grenades. There wasn't much left of the structure either, with its top floors having collapsed on one side. When the same tactic was attempted against the distant Agriculture Building, the Japanese managed to hold out for almost a week until each floor was destroyed and scorched with flamethrowers in turn. The same fate awaited the Finance Building although it took five more days of relentless bombardment until it too was taken. On 3 March, a satisfied Krueger informed MacArthur the battle was done.

The after-action report compiled by Sixth Army on its role in Luzon couldn't have produced a better memorial for what had just befallen the capital of the Philippines. It read: "Thus ended the battle of Manila. The enemy's suicidal defense of the city had cost him 16,665 in counted dead. The number of dead Japanese soldiers disposed of by the enemy or buried in the ruins of destroyed buildings and underground tunnels could not be determined. During the battle of Manila, hardly a building in Manila escaped damage or destruction. Intramuros was a mess of rubble."

Although American casualties were less than ten percent of the enemy's losses, totalling 1,010 KIA after a month, an additional 5,565 were injured and nearly a million Filipinos left homeless. Later accounts speculated that some of the Naval Defence Force did manage to escape from Intramuros while abandoning their arms. As Manila was demilitarized in the following weeks, more than a thousand large-calibre machine guns were collected with the Americans counting 120 artillery pieces used against them.

But for the Philippines there was no end to the fighting, which dragged on for the next few months. Krueger's XIV Corps was tasked with striking deeper into Southern Luzon, beginning with the hills of Antipolo. The bulk of the Shimbu Group was intact, anyway. The rest of the Philippines was still controlled by Japanese forces and it fell on General Eichelberger's Eighth Army to fight on throughout the archipelago. "Everything about the Philippines made magic for me," he later wrote in his memoir. "I had served there as a young officer and the lovely place names rang the bell of memory: they were pure music."

Eichelberger went on to command American forces in the battle for Cebu, another doomed city that met the same fate as Manila, albeit with carnage on a lesser scale. As Japan's total defeat loomed by the summer of 1945, American forces were still struggling to recapture Mindanao, the southernmost landmass in the Philippines. "This was not a battle area like Europe, fought over a hundred times, where every river and valley and eminence is known to the textbooks," Eichelberger wrote of the never-ending island campaigns in the theatre. "But the Southwest Pacific was something else again, this was a section which had never been the scene of a war between great powers."

By August, however, much of the Philippines was under American control once more and the 200,000 soldiers scattered across the archipelago were confident any remaining

Japanese were inclined to surrender. Having lost track of any major concentration of Japanese forces, Eichelberger himself slid back to the pre-war habits that disappeared in December 1941. Assigned a house in Baguio, which was spared from a protracted battle, the general marvelled at the comforts his lodging afforded. "I remember one morning in mid-July 1945 when I awakened at six. It was dark because the house was entirely surrounded by clouds. Twenty minutes later Baguio was bright and shining as the sun came over the mountains. To the east the ranges rose higher and higher, and everywhere were the tall and beautiful pines for which the region is famous," Eichelberger recalled with utmost fondness.

As August drew to a close, XIV Corps' operations in the Cordilleras were tightening the noose around the remaining Japanese under Yamashita. Despite their numbers—rough estimates put total enemy manpower at 40,000 strong—what used to be the Shobu Group responsible for defending the entirety of Northern Luzon was no longer combat effective. Slowly, cautiously, messages were exchanged between Yamashita's clandestine headquarters and General William Gill of the 32nd Infantry Division, also known as the 'Red Arrow Men'. Once the atomic bombs dropped on Hiroshima and Nagasaki between 6 and 9 August hastened Tokyo's ultimate surrender, the capitulation of the Imperial army's left-over divisions in the Philippines was a formality. On 2 September Yamashita and his staff vacated the cave that served as their headquarters and were escorted to Baguio where the Tiger of Malaya surrendered his sword with as much decorum as he could muster. Also in attendance was an unexpected guest, Lieutenant-General Arthur Percival of the British Army, who bore the humiliation of surrendering his entire command to Yamashita in Singapore three years earlier.

But the war wasn't over for the crestfallen, stone-faced Yamashita. His trial began the following month as the highest-ranking Japanese commander in the Philippines who had directed the widespread atrocities committed by his frenzied soldiers. Others in the Japanese occupation were prosecuted as well, including the retired Homma, who led the invasion of the Philippines in 1941 and was held responsible for the Bataan Death March. Even with a team of handpicked American lawyers to defend him, Yamashita was left baffled by the trial arranged by the Military Commission in Manila that spanned eight tense weeks. Unknown to Yamashita at the time, on 9 April a damning report by the XIV Corps Inspector General titled *Investigation of Alleged Atrocities by Members of the Japanese Imperial Forces in Manila and other parts of Luzon, Philippine Islands* was published containing multiple testimonies by Filipino civilians and various expatriates in Manila who were at the receiving end of Japanese brutality. This meant the Yamashita trial was dominated by survivors called in as witnesses and by November they had totalled 286 men and women. While his lawyers still argued that it was the Japanese navy, not an army commander like Yamashita, who was responsible for what happened in Manila, this defence proved inadequate. The Inspector General's report concluded the destruction of the city was a "preconceived plan" assigned to Yamashita.

There was substance to the argument of the Japanese navy's culpability, however. As overall commander of ground forces in the Philippines, Yamashita adopted a similar stratagem

General Yamashita, the once renowned 'Tiger of Malaya', was condemned to hang for Japanese atrocities in Luzon.

as MacArthur in 1941. Manila was to be abandoned and left to the enemy. But Rear Admiral Iwabuchi either rejected this outright or decided to keep fighting when the written orders for an organized retreat failed to arrive from the Shimbu Group HQ. This had to be the most glaring example yet of the discord between the army and navy, IJA and the IJN. On so many occasions in the Pacific theatre, the competing branches exhibited a remarkable talent for non-cooperation. One keen observation made by the Allies is the Japanese never built decent airstrips to the same standards as the American military. This stemmed from a lack of construction equipment and manpower that could be furnished by engineers and soldiers, yet the IJN's air fleets made do without either. As in Leyte Gulf and Manila, the IJN often took the initiative for disastrous strategies while the army was left to fend for itself.

But what Yamashita couldn't be absolved of were the civilians deaths that ballooned in the months when he commanded Japanese forces in the Philippines. In the words of so many witnesses, Japanese soldiers bayoneted unarmed women and children to death with practised ease. Men in particular were often rounded up with their hands tied behind them and when they couldn't be crammed inside dugouts or prison cells and blown to smithereens with grenades, they were either skewered with bayonets or decapitated. There were so many massacres of civilians throughout Luzon, in fact, that the total numbers killed were never counted. These atrocities reached their peak during the battle of Manila and at least six incidents show premeditated war crimes:

- On 1 February, Japanese soldiers stormed De La Salle College along Taft Avenue and murdered 41 civilians, including 16 La Sallian brothers who martyred themselves.
- In mid-February, the Saint Vincent de Paul Parish in Ermita, southeast of Intramuros, was used as a temporary holding area for Filipinos in the neighbourhood. The structure was set on fire, killing several hundred civilians.
- Around the same time, an undisclosed number of residents were gathered in the German Club, a popular venue for expatriates, and locked inside. The building was set on fire and multiple rapes occurred within the property. Bodies were later found mutilated.
- A similar massacre took place on 9 February when hundreds of Malate residents were killed after being locked inside St. Paul's College. Japanese soldiers had lobbed grenades inside the classrooms. It's unclear if they bayoneted any survivors.
- On 10 February Japanese soldiers rampaged in the Philippine National Red Cross Headquarters. Several dozen women and children, including infants, were killed.
- From 7 to 17 February thousands of civilians were forced inside the Philippine General Hospital (PGH) to serve as human shields. Unfortunately, the hospital received multiple hits from American artillery fire until it was captured.

There are numerous accounts like these from the month-long battle. In each of them, Japanese soldiers are described targeting civilians for no discernible reason other than to harm local residents and destroy their property, in what resembled the 'Three Alls' (kill, burn, loot) counterinsurgency doctrine practised in China. They didn't discriminate either and dealt the same cruelty to families rich and poor. The logic behind the mayhem remains a mystery though. Iwabuchi along with the entire MNDF did not survive the fighting and left no records. The only flimsy pretext that can explain the atrocities in Manila was to deprive the Americans of a 'clean' victory. The US Army's force of arms may have won back the capital but the civilian death toll meant the triumph was at least bittersweet, or at worst, pyrrhic. It isn't surprising how, years after the battle, the official death toll is kept at a high estimate of 100,000 killed despite the lack of precise civilian casualty figures from XIV Corps' own documents.

Yamashita himself was convicted on 7 December and imprisoned in Los Baños, the same camp that once held American PoWs, until the date of his execution. A hasty appeal brought to the Supreme Court of the United States argued the Military Commission was an irregular body that couldn't render final judgment on Yamashita. This bought a few more weeks of reprieve but on 4 February 1946, six out of nine judges voted Yamashita's fate was not in the Supreme Court's hands and 20 days later Japan's most famous general was brought to the gallows.

Devastated downtown Manila with a *calesa* (a rickshaw) in the foreground. (Victor Jorgensen (US Navy / NARA 8467430)

On the date of his execution, 23 February 1946, Yamashita left his quarters dressed as a civilian. Accompanying him was the Buddhist monk Morita Shokaku and several other Japanese from the occupation years who were condemned to die. Before his hanging, Yamashita was allowed to share his last words with a living witness. He told the monk he would pray for the Emperor Hirohito, whom the Americans had absolved of any responsibility for the war Japan had lost, and proceeded to his fate. Once the deed was done, his lifeless body was carried away by stretcher for burial. But Yamashita had left behind a single memento. He dictated his 'Last Message to the Japanese People' to Shokaku. In it, the doomed general extolled the virtues of Japan and suggested four principles that should be embraced by the entire nation. Its citizens should subscribe to duty above all else, study science and technology, emancipate Japanese women and let mothers raise their children to be upstanding citizens. But Yamashita also expressed remorse for the war.

"The time has come to atone for my guilt with my death," he said. "However, I do not think that all the crimes for which I am responsible can easily be liquidated simply by my death. Various indelible stains that I left on the history of mankind cannot be offset by the mechanical termination of my life."

9. A COUNTRY IN RUIN

In startling contrast to the bitter independence struggles fought across Asia and Africa that marked the post-war years, the Philippines attained its freedom on the very date set during the establishment of the Commonwealth a decade prior. After peaceful national elections contested between the two main political factions, the Liberal Party and the Nacionalista Party, the statesman and war veteran Manuel Roxas emerged victorious against his opponent, the former vice-president and President-in-Exile Sergio Osmeña. Rather than a study in contrasts, Roxas and the elderly Osmeña shared an unlikely bond: they had both cut their teeth in politics during the run-up to the Commonwealth and witnessed President Quezon's anguish during the early months of 1942. When activated as a reservist officer before Japan's invasion, Major Roxas reported to MacArthur as the USAFFE struggled against Homma's Fourteenth Army in Luzon. In the span of weeks, however, Roxas hastily rose through the ranks until he was made a brigadier general. Having escaped to Mindanao before King's surrender in Bataan, rather than join Quezon

Manuel A. Roxas. (Philippine Presidential Museum and Library)

President José P. Laurel.
(Mainichi Newspaper Office)

in exile he was ordered to stay on and help form the guerrilla resistance, but Roxas was captured by the Japanese shortly after. Instead of condemning him to a PoW camp, Roxas was stripped of his rank and sent home. Once in Manila, like many Filipino civil servants who served the Commonwealth with distinction, Roxas was pressured to join the puppet government led by President José P. Laurel. As if this weren't enough of a black mark on his reputation, in 1945 Roxas and many reluctant 'collaborators' were taken along by Yamashita's stragglers in the vain struggle to hold out against the US Army in the Cordilleras.

But MacArthur's unfailing loyalty to his subordinates meant Roxas, by dint of his prior service with the Commonwealth and brief participation in the local resistance, was soon rehabilitated and groomed for leadership. There are few comparisons to the relationship between the US military and local Filipino elites amid the devastation and euphoria at war's end. Having won the elections by a landslide on 23 April 1946, within a matter of weeks President Manuel Roxas had the supreme responsibility for ushering in the Third Republic on 4 June 1946. To clarify the political evolution of the Philippines until that point, the First Republic was established by General Emilio Aguinaldo, who had barely reached his late 20s, in 1898 but was soon crushed during the ensuing American conquest. (It deserves mention how an ageing Aguinaldo lived long enough to witness the birth of the Commonwealth and endure the occupation years and all the major post-independence upheavals until his death in 1964.) The Second Republic was an anomaly cobbled together by the Japanese with Laurel as its titular head of state in 1943. True and irrevocable Philippine independence was embodied by the Third Republic under Roxas, whose platform involved establishing so many linkages between the former colonial authority and its overseas possession, be it generous loans, grants and allowing the US military to remain at Clark and in Subic. So the Republic of the Philippines came to exist under the unfailing guardianship of the world's first true superpower.

But even before his term could begin President Roxas shouldered a burden equally daunting and severe. Perhaps it was too great for any single Filipino politician, much less a fledgling administration with hardly any resources at its disposal, to lead a reconstruction on the scale needed by the Philippines in the late 1940s. No amount of rhetorical talent and spin could have softened the dispiriting assessment Roxas delivered to the legislature about the country's circumstances a full month before independence on 4 July. On his very first State of the Nation Address, or SONA, which he was obligated to give each year, Roxas acknowledged the enormity of the task ahead. "The very hall in which I've sat is a tragic testimonial to what has occurred here," he told his audience of congressmen. "We are reduced to convening in a former Japanese schoolhouse while the proud legislative building we had built before the war lies in ugly, ghastly ruin."

Roxas was referring to the Legislature Building built on the corner of Luneta. Like every administrative structure in the vicinity of the historic park, it too had been hardened with Japanese machine-gun nests and booby traps. In the thick of the fighting in late February the upper floors collapsed after receiving so many direct hits from howitzer and tank shells. The whole structure was rehabilitated with foreign aid and is known today as the National Museum of Fine Art.

But Roxas's SONA, with its appalling detail and matter-of-factness, made for a sobering presentation. "Most of our government functions are carried out in crowded, temporary or bombed-out structures," Roxas said. Pausing for breath, he finally admitted his most pressing concern: "But the central fact of our condition is the tragic destruction of the productive economy."

It was this minor revelation—apparent to all who were in attendance—that showed the bittersweet quality of the republic's newfound freedom. Roxas's historic SONA was held on 3 June 1946. The battle of Manila ended on 3 March 1945 and combat operations in the Philippines lasted until Yamashita's surrender on 3 September that same year. This meant in mid-1946, with the Cold War's chill spreading over the world, the Filipino state-to-be was still coming to grips with the scale of its recovery. Roxas also had a point by lamenting the "productive economy". Four decades of American colonial rule meant the Philippines had progressed as an agricultural hub with an economy fuelled by abaca, copra and sugar exports. The intervening war years destroyed everything. Added to the woeful litany was the crippling shortage of any government revenue, ruinous inflation caused by a surplus of useless 'guerrilla currency', and the absence of law and order. Roxas didn't hesitate to claim 300,000 firearms were then in the hands of rogue elements. The president bemoaned the unusable mines of gold and other precious metals, the lack of sawmills for processing timber and the looming food shortage that could only be remedied by importing rice from Siam (Thailand). Compensation and pensions for 200,000 Filipino USAFFE veterans and the guerrilla resistance remained in limbo—would they or wouldn't they receive benefits from the American government? Without a shadow of doubt, there was no end to the republic's ills.

To his audience's relief, Roxas did offer a few immediate remedies. The Trade Rehabilitation Act and the War Damage Act were two pending bills that, in Roxas's words, could revive the economy by insuring the material losses of American enterprises in the Philippines. Another helpful piece of legislation called the Bell Trade Act passed less than a month later and granted the United States an inordinate role in the Philippines' private sector, whose managers were usually Americans anyway. Aside from new laws, a loan worth 1.2 billion pesos, whose value was pegged to the US dollar, was under discussion between Manila and Washington DC as well. The first portion required a year-long subsidy totalling 800 million pesos. The remaining 500 million pesos would come from the Export-Import Bank of the United States.

This over-dependence on a former colonizer does seem like the Philippines only had a façade of sovereignty. But what choice did Roxas and a traumatized nation have? Come Independence Day on 4 July, Roxas was all praise for his gracious benefactors. "Should we in the Philippines disdain the support of this modern Colossus whose might is the hope and strength of the world? No free nation today can, to its advantage, scoff and snarl at the United States, whose broad shoulders bear the awful weight of world peace ... Subtract the influence of the United States from the rest of the world," Roxas declared, "and the answer is chaos."

Noble as his intentions were, patriotic might have been his vision for the country, President Roxas was an ill-fated head of state. His time in office lasted a year and ten months before he died from a heart attack after delivering a speech at Clark Field, one of the most contentious locations during the war. The suddenness of the tragedy may have had its origins during the war, when Roxas's brief imprisonment in Mindanao left him susceptible to hypertension. His unexpected death propelled Vice-President Elpidio Quirino to take the reigns of leadership and organize a new administration, a task fraught with problems. On top of the frustrating complexities involved with charting the republic's course was a Communist revolt in Central Luzon by the Huks, whose origins as an anti-Japanese partisan movement endeared them to the peasantry. In summation, the two decades following the battle of Manila were a difficult period for the Philippines and Japan's own unwillingness to pay reparations—during the 1950s it began donating tools and machinery—meant the sole financial recourse available to every Filipino leader was either grants or loans from abroad. Perhaps the uncomfortable friction caused by nascent patriotism tempered by awful economic realities led to a welcome mythologizing. A common belief propagated by the post-war generation of Filipinos was the Philippines attaining a measure of advancement and prosperity second only to Japan. But this is rubbish. The World Bank's own measurement of the Philippine economy in the last 50 years shows Gross National Product (GNP) stood at $6.6 billion in 1960. This trailed Japan's own GNP then by a wide margin and it was Communist China, not the Philippines, that was the second largest economy in the Asia-Pacific at the time.

Another myth that deserves a rightful beat-down is the enduring legend of a 'Yamashita Treasure'. According to the dodgy accounts that became fodder for newspapers after the war, vast quantities of gold bullion were transported to Luzon in late 1944 just when Yamashita arrived in the Philippines. In the course of several months the beleaguered general and his troops managed to deposit the hoard, whose size and scale was never verified, across multiple locations. Yamashita himself never spilled the beans on these hidden riches although the late dictator Ferdinand Marcos promoted the falsehood that he built his ill-gotten fortune by retrieving a golden statue of the Buddha. To this day, little of this 'treasure' has been found anywhere in the Philippines although its bare details are irresistible copy for clickbait websites and awful pseudo-documentaries found on YouTube.

Putting it bluntly, the 'Yamashita Treasure' is complete nonsense and a disservice to the millions of Filipinos who suffered under Japan's pitiless occupation. To be specific, none of the so-called details surrounding the legend make sense. Yamashita arrived in the Philippines in October 1944 with orders to resist the Americans for as long as possible. Sending mysterious cargoes of gold supposedly plundered from China and elsewhere to a theatre being recaptured by MacArthur's forces is illogical. Neither was Japan's air and maritime freight in 1944 up to the task of delivering bullion since their logistical reach had withered from attrition. It is equally stupid assuming Yamashita carried out a secret operation to hide tons of loot throughout Luzon when his entire command was falling apart and motor transport was in short supply. To finally lay the myth to rest, captured Japanese soldiers and airmen, who were exhaustively debriefed by American interrogators, never once divulged the existence of gold hidden anywhere in the Philippines; neither did Yamashita during his rigorous cross-examination before he was sentenced to death. The present volume is an account of a climactic event that impacted countless lives and shaped a nation's history. I would rather the world learn to appreciate the ordeal my country went through in the bitter struggle to defeat Japan's militarist empire than indulge balderdash like the Yamashita Treasure.

But there are authentic legends that did originate from the war. Authentic in the sense of past occurrences shaping the present. These do not involve tantalizing piffle but actual people who lived through the events described in previous chapters and went on to influence modern Filipino society. Of course I know who they are, because I was born and raised in the world they helped create. Foremost is Joseph Ralph McMicking, an American Scot who built the real estate empire still owned by one of the Philippines wealthiest families—the Ayalas. McMicking, or 'Uncle Joe' as his nephews called him, was born in the Philippines and married the heiress Mercedes Zobel y Roxas, whose parents owned the *hacienda* known as San Pedro de Macati, that was conveniently spread between Nielson Field and Fort McKinley. When war broke out McMicking, like so many other well-heeled young men at the time, joined MacArthur's staff and was assigned to Colonel Charles Willoughby's intelligence unit. When MacArthur famously waded ashore at Leyte, McMicking was among those walking behind him except the best-known photograph from the event left him out of frame. Unfortunately, he left behind his wife, his mother and four siblings in 1942. It wasn't until war's end when McMicking reunited with his beloved Mercedes but, except for a surviving brother, his family was murdered by the Japanese in the battle of Manila.

The childless McMickings spent the post-war years carefully developing their *haci-enda*, the sprawling estates favoured by wealthy families during the American colonial period, and the city of Makati that rose from it earned a reputation for its high rises and cleanliness, supplanting the Escolta as the country's financial hub known as the Central Business District or CDB. Under McMicking's guidance the Ayala Corporation grew into one of the Philippines' largest conglomerates by the time he retired in 1967. Through it all, Uncle Joe remained an elusive figure working in almost total secrecy managing office blocks and suburban communities whose sprawl covered any evidence of the relentless combat in and around Manila in 1945.

Nielson Field, for example, has disappeared under a maze of high rises. Its last remaining vestige, a lone control tower, is a landmark housing a library. There's not a single trace of the Genko Line that blocked the route to Fort McKinley and so bedevilled the tireless 11th Airborne. Spread over the same grass-covered meadows once littered with dugouts and Japanese machine-gun nests is the Ayala Corporation's pet project, the Bonifacio Global City or BGC, where I've spent more than a few evenings dining out with friends. The name of this development is borrowed from a local army base and it was built to attract the corporate set who needed glass-covered office towers with decent views and global amenities. Meanwhile, the acreage of nearby Fort McKinley is now just 'the Fort' with its endless restaurants and mixed-use dwellings.

Another individual who attained the same stature as McMicking was the Spaniard Andres Soriano. What isn't usually emphasized about the American colonial period and the early years of the Commonwealth was the prestige enjoyed by Spanish families in Manila who stayed behind after the earlier colonial regime disappeared. President Quezon himself was of Spanish descent and his most trusted aide-de-camp, Colonel Manuel Nieto, came from a landowning Spanish family but he chose public service as a vocation. Soriano, however, fought valiantly in Bataan and joined MacArthur's escape to Australia where he acquired American citizenship and served in every campaign of the South West Pacific Area. He returned to the Philippines during the Sixth Army's arrival in Lingayen but it was never ascertained if he got caught up in the battle of Manila a few weeks later. After the war, Soriano devoted his energies to expanding the San Miguel Brewery and its success rubbed off on the Soriano family's other iconic venture, Philippine Air Lines or PAL. When he died Soriano left a corporate empire built on San Miguel's world famous beer and one of Asia's best airlines.

There are countless stories of the same breadth and scope as McMicking and Soriano, two ex-US Army veterans who reaped rewards from victory after the Philippines was liberated in 1945. Surely, the experiences of women matter too and the suffering they endured in Japanese captivity deserves a lasting memorial. This is why the monument to the battle of Manila built inside Intramuros depicts a mother clutching her lifeless infant atop a huddle of men and women in anguished repose. Unlike the palatial monument on Corregidor to celebrate the USAFFE's doomed efforts at resisting the Japanese, the macabre symbolism of the Intramuros Memorare is intentionally far less grandiose. While the Philippine government does its part raising awareness about the victims of the massacres that took place in 1945, questions persist. For example, the motivations of the Rikusentai have never been explored by official historians, leaving them as one-dimensional villains in the history books. Worse, while 100,000 civilians are reported to have died in the battle of Manila, there's neither a complete ledger nor a database for names and places, an embarrassing contrast to American casualties in Manila. There were definitely multiple incidents of war crimes during the liberation, but a rigorous accounting for the dead has never materialized. This represents a loss to heritage and history not just for the Philippines, but Japan and the United States as well.

I do know of one more individual who may have witnessed Manila's destruction firsthand. I visited his house, in fact, a few short months before he died from a heart attack. I will never forget entering the small apartment of Pablo S. Gomez, or Mr. Gomez as

The Memorare is a haunting reminder of the horrors that swept the Philippine capital in 1945. (Judgefloro)

I would rather call him, one morning in 2010. I was still a university student then and wanted to learn about his years as one of the highest-paid writers in the country. During the 1950s, the absence of television meant Filipinos patronized *komiks*, the locally made comic books filled with stories of every conceivable genre, and Mr. Gomez's talents then were considered formidable. Not only was he a trailblazer of the medium but young and successful at a time when publishing in the vernacular, rather than English, was considered low class. Still an unrepentant chain smoker in his 80s, Mr. Gomez kept a manual typewriter on a small desk in his living room as if it were a shrine. He told me the sounds it made when he hammered out a script, and he was always working on another script, reassured him. By the sheer force of his imagination Mr. Gomez shaped the *komiks* industry as an author, an entrepreneur, a talent scout, a publisher, and when his printing house folded he seeded local cinema with some of its most memorable blockbusters. But in the course of listening to his reminiscences—I had visited as a fan hungry for a connection to a mythical past I held sacred—Mr. Gomez mentioned his childhood in passing. He was born to a poor family before the war and vividly recalled being pressganged by the Japanese as a labourer. He didn't elaborate on this particular memory and I didn't want to dwell on what sounded like an upsetting topic. Was Mr. Gomez a hostage during the battle of Manila? What did the Japanese make him do, and do to him?

Months after our morning chat in his living room I learned from the news that Mr. Gomez had died; he was a legend in some circles after all, and I realized a precious link to a bygone era had disappeared forever. The regret over not revisiting his storied life haunts me to this day. Mr. Gomez deserved better.

Manila and its sister cities are full of personal sagas threaded with hope and despair. I've spent my entire life in the sprawl of Metro Manila and witnessed its grime and poverty co-existing with an urban jungle's frenetic pace and dizzying consumerism. I've circled the walls of Intramuros and measured their impenetrable thickness that only the largest howitzer shells could breach. I've stood on Fort Santiago's battlements, far above the subterranean dungeons where the Japanese slaughtered hundreds of prisoners, to watch the Pasig river's murky current flow by. The Far Eastern University and the University of Santo Tomas, those two vital landmarks at the beginning of the struggle to liberate Manila, are mundane edifices I ignore on long commutes. I'm no stranger to the sparkling horizon of Manila Bay at dawn and dusk. Entire portions of the city form a backdrop to my own life. But the nightmare that unfolded in the first three months of 1945 is a testament to human suffering that must never be forgotten by Filipinos. It will always matter because it was the blank slate from which a new country was reborn and rebuilt. I'm tempted to reminisce on a personal connection to the battle. My grandparents were married on 5 August 1943 and settled down in Legarda, an affluent neighbourhood between Malacañang Palace and the University of Santo Tomas, which meant they were perilously close to the fighting that took place in February 1945. I wonder how they managed to survive the maelstrom that almost tore their world apart. How did they?

EPILOGUE: FACING A STRATEGIC CONUNDRUM

On 14 August 2018 the American embassy in Manila announced it had donated a $15 million SABIR to the Philippine Air Force. The Special Airborne Mission Installation and Response kit manufactured by Airdyne comprised twin modules on either side of a C-130 transport's airframe, specifically located behind the landing gear. Its purpose was to help the crew take surveillance footage over vast distances. While the occasion was hailed as the latest collaboration in the long-lasting alliance between Manila and Washington, less emphasized was the gesture's significance. The air force's C-130s were the only assets that had the range to fly over the Spratly Islands and back: the C-130 with a SABIR was a spy plane needed in the South China Sea.

It begs the question: How is the battle of Manila relevant to the Philippines' territorial crisis today?

Over the decades, what originated as a long simmering tiff over sandbars and islets between China and its estranged former ally Vietnam metastasized into a convoluted struggle over the faraway Spratlys involving five nearby countries: Brunei, Indonesia, the Philippines, Malaysia and Taiwan. Since 2012, however, Chinese ships loaded with dredging equipment and their crews have been hard at work reclaiming and then constructing buildings over specific features in the Spratlys. When the Hague judged China's broad claims over the area null in July 2016 this had no effect on the seven permanent bases it had established. Should non-Chinese aircraft or ships approach these locations they are vigorously warned and threatened over radio.

Even as the Philippines reached out in friendship to China—President Rodrigo Duterte visited Beijing in October 2016 and declared fealty to his hosts—the military has followed another set of priorities. In July 2018, a full month before the American embassy's SABIR announcement, two Philippine Navy vessels—a Landing Platform Dock and a former US Coast Guard cutter repurposed as a frigate—sailed for Hawaii to join a flotilla of warships from the Indian and Japanese navies on their way to the same event: RIMPAC,* the world's largest multilateral naval exercise.

During the previous year the full strength of the Philippine military was thrown against radical Islamists who had seized Marawi, a predominantly Muslim city in the province of Lanao del Sur. This was the latest showdown in an unbroken civil war that had plagued the southernmost island of Mindanao since the 1970s. In scenes that eerily recalled the carnage and destruction in Manila 72 years before, buildings were reduced to pockmarked edifices. Through the months of grinding combat in Marawi, US assistance remained steadfast as replenishment flights of ammunition and guided bombs

---

* Rim of the Pacific Exercise.

kept Filipino soldiers, marines, policemen and pilots fighting until the last terrorists were killed in late October. Although China offered token assistance as well, this was insignificant compared to American largesse.

In the months following Marawi the co-dependence of the American and Filipino militaries grew stronger, contrary to Duterte's own disdain for an alliance that he considered exploitative. But try as he might, there has never been a Filipino head of state who has succeeded in terminating the bond between the two countries. Throughout 2018, in fact, the US Navy's aircraft carriers docked in Manila Bay every quarter before embarking on Freedom of Navigation Operations, or FONOPS—demonstrations meant to negate China's claims over the Spratlys. As the year drew to a close one of these trips was accompanied by Japanese warships. Beijing seethed.

Drones, propeller-driven patrol planes, annual exercises involving marines … Washington's generosity to Manila is consistent and dependable. When Duterte bragged about a Russian offer to sell submarines to the Philippine Navy, he was quickly shown a letter from the State Department that suggested he buy F-16 multirole fighters instead. Clearly and without any trace of doubt, the Philippines is not allowed to drift from America's orbit. This pattern of interaction, equally cooperative and transactional, has repeated itself decade after decade since the Philippine Commonwealth. Now it makes even more sense why MacArthur insisted that recapturing the Philippines was vital to defeating Japan rather than a multi-pronged assault on Formosa. The underlying strategic logic was to seize the island of Luzon, together with the rest of the Philippines, essential for controlling the maritime supply routes for sustaining a war against Japan. These routes were located in the tranquil South China Sea, in the narrow strait between Formosa and Fujian and in the East China Sea leading to Japan's southernmost islands. Hence, Luzon along with the rest of the Philippines had to be in American hands once more.

The situation today is different. Japan is a firm US ally as are South Korea, Taiwan and the Philippines. The problem is China, whose economy has grown to the second largest in the world, and its inscrutable yet menacing ambitions. If all the evidence of island-building and provocative flights suggests that China, like Japan in the early and mid-20th century, aspires to impose its own warped 'co-prosperity sphere' over East Asia, this explains why it keeps undermining Taiwan, why it keeps reinforcing its artificial islands in the Spratlys, why it feuds with Japan over barren rocks, why it tacitly supports North Korea's bizarre regime. This kind of behaviour suggests a conflict with the US is inevitable and the stakes are remarkably the same as in the last World War. Who shall have dominion of the Pacific Ocean?

The struggle that ensued between Imperial Japan and America between 1941 and 1945 devastated the Philippines, whose fledgling government had no grandiose aspirations of its own. Likewise, if a showdown between China and the US is soon to erupt, the same terrible fate would befall my country.

Bear in mind, the island of Luzon is between the South China Sea and Guam, where the US Air Force has an airbase, the US Marine Corps a training base and the US Navy a submarine base. If the Great Sino-American War breaks out over Taiwan, chances are the ensuing air battles, missile barrages and naval clashes will occur in the vicinity of Luzon. Regardless of how prepared Manila is for such a scenario, if US aircraft seek shelter or replenish at Clark Air Base or any aistrip near Manila, this is an open invitation for China to expeditiously deal with the matter. And if a US-led coalition, like an 'Indo-Pacific Alliance +,' is what China must confront, then the Philippines must be seized immediately. It's too close to the South China Sea and a short flight away from the mainland, which means it can't be allowed to be used as somebody else's forward base, making it a priority target by geographical default.

During World War II, Japan occupied the Philippines to secure control of Southeast Asia and nearby maritime routes. In the next global conflict, the aggressor must secure the Philippines to 'break out' of its territorial waters and prosecute the war deeper in the Pacific Ocean. The lesson here is, no matter who is trying to control Asia, subduing the Philippines is essential.

At last we arrive at a final answer for the original question. It's the strategic importance of the Philippines that makes the battle of Manila an enduring lesson for today and tomorrow. Revisiting the battle is equally valuable for the clues it imparts on a sinister pattern in Philippine history. Indeed, there are no shortage of books and research on the events surrounding Manila's liberation in 1945. But what these never acknowledge is the intrinsic value of the location: why controlling Manila was a prerequisite for controlling the rest of the Philippines.

The destruction of Manila in 1945 wasn't the first instance it was almost completely destroyed. Barring natural calamities such as earthquakes, every major conflict in Philippine history has always climaxed with a battle for Manila. In February 1899 the fighting between the American Expeditionary Forces, the volunteer regiments mobilized for the Spanish-American War that had concluded the year before and the Filipino revolutionaries who were determined to establish an independent state, left the outlying suburbs such as San Juan and Tondo in ruin. The Americans ultimately prevailed then as they did against Japan 46 years later.

Perusing my country's historical records unearths more bitter lessons. Manila was first put to the torch in 1572 when a small army commanded by the Basque conquistador, Miguel Lopez de Legazpi, drove out the local ruler, Raja Humabon, from his humble fortress at the mouth of a lush river that became known as the Pasig. The imposition of a permanent settlement, the Intramuros and a new centralized governing regime for the islands dubbed the Kingdom of New Castile ushered in the colonial era that lasted until 1898. The justification for the conquest then was twofold. Foremost was establishing a new trade route that would swell the Spanish Empire's coffers after the debacle of the armada it had sent against England. A secondary goal was a foothold in Asia where further conquests could be launched, either through force or by proselytizing the Catholic faith.

But the Spanish colonial regime never fully controlled the archipelago that became Filipinas as threats from within and without always undermined Manila's rule. A few years after defeating Humabon, the unprepared garrison in Manila withstood a siege by a Chinese pirate warlord whose army had marched across the northern plains with impunity. Then, in 1591, Spain's grip on the Philippines was once again in jeopardy when Japan's reigning Shogun, Toyotomi Hideyoshi, demanded tribute. Failing to meet his terms risked a full-scale invasion. Much to the relief of the Spanish residents in Manila the Shogun never carried through.

The first hundred years of Spanish rule over the Philippines were far from tranquil. When endless pirate raids on Christian settlements weren't straining the *Gobernador Heneral*'s resources, there was a major conflict in Europe that brought invasions by the Dutch and the Portuguese. In 1762 the British East India Company did their part for king and country during the Seven Years' War by sending a fleet to attack Manila. The army they assembled had Englishmen in command of Indian sepoys who were renowned for their battlefield prowess. The Spanish, in circumstances that form a recurring theme during their long and troubled occupation of the Philippines, were ill-prepared for the naval onslaught and little could be done to protect Manila Bay and the Intramuros. Luckily, rather than replace the Spanish governors as the new colonial administrators, the British East India Company withdrew its forces within a year.

Back again to 1898. In late April the US Navy's Asiatic Squadron under Commodore George Dewey was visiting Hong Kong but quickly departed for the Philippines. Arriving in Manila Bay just hours before daybreak on May 1, Dewey's ships had no trouble finding the Spanish flotilla at anchor in Cavite that was subsequently reduced with ease. The first volunteer regiments of the US Army soon landed on the unguarded shoreline east of the Pasig river. After the Philippine-American War the same stretch of beach was paved over and named Dewey Boulevard. Today it's known as Roxas Boulevard, after the first president of the Third Republic. I recall walking its length one sweltering midday in the last week of September to reach a 'defence' exhibition at a nearby venue where arms dealers from Israel, the European Union, South Korea, Russia and the United States had erected towering booths for showcasing their products, where it was hardly a surprise to find scale models of various submarines and warships on display.

Legazpi in 1572, the British in 1762, the Americans in 1898 and finally the Japanese in 1941. There's a pattern here. In each instance the defenders, even with the local population and dry land on their side, always failed to repulse the enemy. With the exception of thwarting numerous Dutch forays in the 1700s, each foreign invader who sought to rule Manila along with the rest of the Philippines succeeded. Of course, the Japanese army and navy achieved the same on a spectacular scale in May 1942 after compelling the last holdouts in Corregidor to surrender. This had to be the lowest point in the military history of the United States as its generals and soldiers were marched into captivity. General Homma, just like General Yamashita with the British in Singapore, was the first modern Asian military leader to inflict total defeat on the American military in a conventional war. But Homma and Yamashita were doomed to ignominy: both were arrested, prosecuted and then executed in the Philippines after the war.

If the Philippines always succumbs to external aggression, as it did in almost every turning point in its recorded history, it does makes one think whether Filipino nationalism is ill-founded. My country spent the decades of independence that followed World War II struggling to balance economic development with an equitable democracy. The course was always troublesome and the dictatorship of Ferdinand Marcos from 1972 until 1986 inflicted grievous wounds on both prerogatives. Worse, the historical facts that underpin this damning cycle of war and occupation reveal the notion of an enduring Filipino state to be a mirage: it never existed.

From Legazpi to the day after Pearl Harbor, every time great naval powers fought among themselves the question of who gains access to Asia and its resources is decided in the Philippines and its nearby waters. Recall how the initial contest between the Spanish and Portuguese in the 16th century meant endless skirmishing from the Bay of Bengal to Luzon. In the 20th century, when Japan was the undisputed military heavyweight of East Asia with the region's strongest navy, it successfully trounced the British, Dutch, French and American forces in less than half a year.

That the ultimate demise of the Japanese navy happened in the Philippine Sea and Leyte Gulf shows how important the maritime routes surrounding my country are, their true value having such immeasurable necessity in the eyes of cold-blooded grand strategists. The infernal logic they must accept dictates that the Philippines is extremely hard to defend yet too valuable to be lost. MacArthur and Yamashita had the misfortune of witnessing this logic at play when they both tried holding Luzon against a superior enemy.

If I applied the same criteria to Asia's geopolitics today, the resulting picture is chilling. With 'great' navies as prerequisites and the inevitability of open warfare a given, the present climate fits the same recurring pattern that has doomed the Philippines for generations. The current theatre is a familiar one that took shape after World War II. The US Navy remains the guarantor of the Asia-Pacific and the lesser navies maintained by Japan, Australia and India are now aligned with it to form a quadrilateral bloc for discouraging Chinese expansion. The modest navies of South Korea and Taiwan enjoy a remarkable inter-operability with the US Navy as well.

Unfortunately, the naval strength of the Philippines is dismal and its present state sharply contrasts with its counterparts in Indonesia, Malaysia, Singapore and Vietnam. But all these local navies are dwarfed by the rapid expansion of China's own fleets guarding its northern, eastern and southern seas. The Chinese PLAN or PLA-N[*] are now on track to have at least six aircraft carriers by the late 2020s, half in the 100,000-ton range, putting them on the same scale as the Nimitz and Ford classes. In 2018, the Pentagon estimated PLAN has 64 diesel-electric submarines and the total will keep rising together with newer classes of nuclear-powered submarines. The world's largest guided-missile destroyers in terms of displacement are made in Chinese shipyards that launch them four times a year. These join an already daunting assembly of PLAN destroyers and frigates loaded with cruise missiles. In a true signal of intent, PLAN is increasing its fledgling marine corps to 100,000 personnel with weapons surpassing those used by the United States Marine Corps.

---

[*]   People's Liberation Army Navy.

On 12 April 2018 one of the strangest naval demonstrations ever undertaken by PLAN took place in the South China Sea. A convoy of 48 ships escorted by low-flying bombers and submarines held a 'parade' viewed by President Xi Jinping attired in digital battle dress. In his speech delivered aboard a destroyer, Xi praised the navy's strength and encouraged its sailors to always be prepared for war. The Chinese leader's message grows darker in hindsight. As the PLAN and the US Navy keep provoking each other amid an escalating Sino-American 'trade war', whose goal is to hurt China's exports in order to slow its economy, historical perspective grows increasingly ominous. The onset of World War II in the Pacific had its origins in punitive US sanctions on Japan's access to fuel and raw materials. If America and its allies are on the brink of war with China, it looks like I'm condemned to live through another turning point in Philippine history.

As the pattern of conflict I describe reveals, the naval powers who vie for Asia-Pacific domination will end up either attacking or defending the Philippines, with catastrophic results for the Filipino people. The last time it happened nearly a tenth of the local population was killed and the destruction reached an unimaginable scale. Post-war recovery and the burden of developing an independent state meant Filipino leaders had little choice but to solicit aid and loans from abroad. President Roxas understood this in 1946 and so did President Duterte when his term began in July 2016. For the sake of domestic peace while the country built itself up, the Philippines remained under the US's security umbrella. Now that Beijing looks poised to challenge Washington's role in Asia and elsewhere, the Philippines adapts. Just as the staunchly pro-American President Quezon visited Japan and paid homage to its Emperor before the war, Duterte and his cabinet have almost contorted themselves appeasing China's leader with promises of friendship and requests for aid. But the Philippines hasn't reneged on its loyalty to the US, which is why the American embassy is generous with its promises of material aid.

If the Philippines is always doomed to be contested by naval forces, the only sensible recourse is preparing for the country's defence with the help of trusted allies. Unlike so many past instances, hostile navies can never be allowed to approach Luzon and must be deterred by a combination of aircraft and shore-based missiles linked with overlapping radar sites. The government should abandon its habit of subordinating the yearly military budget to education. Let both be raised high enough for public universities to expand STEM courses that will feed research and engineering talent into state-owned enterprises tasked with supplying the military. The Spanish, American and finally Japanese armies that tried to defend the Philippines from attack always failed because of ill-conceived plans and inferior equipment. Much to my disappointment, I recognize the present state of the Armed Forces of the Philippines (AFP) as falling into the same pattern. It doesn't have a well-practised doctrine for territorial defence and its present inventory is dismal. To make an awful comparison, the Japanese had thousands of combat aircraft and thousands more anti-aircraft guns to defend the Philippines in 1945—they failed anyway. Approaching the third decade of the 21st century, my country's armed forces have no genuine multirole fighter jets and no credible ground-based air defences save for a few large-calibre automatic cannons. I happen to be aware of the military's acquisition plans in the coming years. Until the arrival of two brand-new frigates ordered from South Korea, there are no viable air defences to protect Manila or the Lingayen Gulf or any major city in the Visayas and Mindanao. Knowing full well how Japan's medium bombers indiscriminately pummelled Luzon in late 1941, I have to remind myself I should be upset about this possible scenario repeating itself. The Philippine military does have plans to buy drones, diesel-electric submarines, radars and surface-to-air missiles at some point; I hope it's sooner rather than later. If the Philippines continues to exist as a republic with its national identity and geographical form intact, then territorial defence is an almost sacred endeavour. But hindsight should be the one imparting hard lessons here. Whenever the Philippines succumbed to foreign conquest, be it Spanish or American, every facet of the local culture underwent some change that suited the colonizer's goals. The Imperial Japanese Army were here too briefly so they couldn't accomplish the same. Yet post-war Japan is a generous benefactor that has always lavished the Philippines with investments and loans. It's not surprising how its cultural exports and consumer brands are wholeheartedly embraced by Filipinos and I can personally vouch for so many *things* Japanese that are permanent fixtures in my life, from toy robots to a cherished college friend and little nephews who are a quarter Japanese. The point I want to make is when I discuss Japanese war crimes that happened two generations ago, I'm exploring recent history rather than condemning an entire nation. Besides, the same preferences Filipinos have for Japanese merchandise applies equally to Chinese and South Korean material influences. So powerful are the cultural links between the Philippines and East Asia today that I sometimes wonder if interpersonal norms and social traits from the region are being gently absorbed by Filipinos, but I'm neither a historian nor a sociologist.

I am and intend to remain a Filipino citizen, albeit with an admittedly reserved patriotism, and I care about my country's future as an independent state. If revisiting Manila's destruction in 1945 has taught me anything, it's the value of freedom and liberty for all Filipinos. In the past, the aggression of powerful countries deprived my countrymen of both because an awful strategic conundrum was at work. This must never happen again. The conundrum needs to be resolved for the sake of all Filipinos.

SOURCES

How does anyone go about a subject as dismal as the battle of Manila? As made clear by the preceding chapters, a huge civilian death toll is its enduring legacy instead of breathtaking martial heroism. Unless they can access the National Archives in Maryland, researchers have a wealth of secondary material on the Philippines during World War II at their fingertips thanks to the worldwide web. But primary sources are harder to find for a number of reasons. The Philippine government, for example, doesn't have extensive archives for storing the masses of documents that survived the war. Trudging off to the National Library, whose present address is located near the site of the worst fighting during the battle of Manila, and browsing its shelves isn't a method I recommend either.

To be fair, there are firsthand accounts written by Filipinos, or their biographers, about the war but these are mostly out of print. A lucky find for me, however, was *Roxas: The Story of A Great Filipino and of the Political Era in which He Lived* by Marcial P. Lichauco, who was a close friend of the book's subject. While it hardly dealt with the battle of Manila the contents furnished enough details to capture the pitiless occupation years between1942 and 1945. I found this particular gem in that sublime repository, the Internet Archive or archive.org.

The assiduous use of archive.org's search bar conjured four priceless tomes on the war and the events leading to Manila. Foremost was *Triumph in the Philippines* by Robert Ross Smith that serves as the companion volume to *The Fall of the Philippines* by Louis Morton. Accompanying these are two intimidating compendiums rich in dates, facts and locations. *Reports of General MacArthur: Japanese Operations in the Southwest Pacific Area* Volume I–Volume II provide a wealth of maps alongside laborious assessments for every operation in the Philippines. The memoir *General Douglas MacArthur: Reminiscences* provided lots of useful first-person accounts to accompany the tactical literature. Another compressed doorstopper of the same magnitude bears an equally laborious title, *Sixth United States Army Report of the Luzon Campaign: 9 January 1945 to 30 June 1945*, and combines typewritten pages that form an accessible narrative for the Luzon campaign. The accompanying photos in the Sixth Army Report are nice too, if rather small.

But the works of Morton and Smith deserve my highest praise. Taken together, a good several months of careful reading went by just to absorb the necessary background for familiarizing myself with World War II in the Asia-Pacific, specifically what transpired in the Philippines. Serious scholars and avid military history readers who wish to learn about the battle of Manila via a blow-by-blow account are well-served by Smith's *Triumph in the Philippines* that chronicles the entire campaign to liberate my country, from Leyte Gulf to Yamashita's surrender. But I'm more inclined to praise Morton's work because I felt immense pressure describing the Japanese invasion and occupation succinctly in the opening chapters of this book. His retelling allowed me to internalize the needed background information on the USAFFE's humiliating defeat until I felt comfortable enough with the facts and details. I also marvelled at how equally desperate and foolish the Americans were in their plans to resist the Japanese onslaught. This is why I made it a point to mention that the loss of Bataan and then Corregidor stand as the biggest military defeats ever inflicted on the United States. Not only did its military suffer appalling human and material losses, with untold numbers of GIs shipped to Japan as slave labour, but thousands of its own citizens were condemned to captivity as a result. There is a handful of sensational titles that offer individual perspectives on Bataan and Corregidor. These weren't essential to my own research on the battle but I dipped into them anyway since they illustrate lives put under extreme duress in wartime and contrast the glowing heroism that too many other books grant the US military in the Pacific theatre.

Colonel E. B. Miller's *Bataan Uncensored* is a decent memoir on the battle and its travails from a veteran who was in the thick of it. The language is colourful and the narrative offers a welcome blend of just-the-facts retelling and bitter observations as the situation in the peninsula became increasingly desperate. The author's time in captivity is included too which is useful for corroborating other accounts such as Russel Brines's *Until They Eat Stones*. In his book, Brines shares a civilian's perspective on the fall of the Philippines and his brief imprisonment in the dreaded University of Santo Tomas. Royal Arch Gunnison's *So Sorry, No Peace* is a shockingly similar book, complete with chapters on Santo Tomas and a subsequent exile. A worthy companion volume to Brines's and Gunnison's wartime tell-alls is Claire 'High Pockets' Phillips's *Manila Espionage* that deserves a place in any Asian-centric World War II reading list for its value as a memoir of a female spy in an occupied country; as a testament to the culture and nightlife of Manila before, during and at the war's end; and a useful text on the ridiculous art of intelligence and counter-intelligence. Phillips's own credentials as a spy couldn't be more simultaneously authentic and unbelievable. For reasons that are still baffling to readers in the 21st century, Phillips and her daughter travelled across the Pacific and arrived in Manila barely three months before Pearl Harbor. Apparently, she wanted to turn a fresh page after a contentious divorce and Manila's bar scene at the time always welcomed a new starlet. This despite the worrisome sense of an imminent war and a strict curfew being enforced by the USAFFE over Manila. Phillips ended up in a whirlwind romance with an American soldier who was subsequently killed and this set her on the path to becoming a spy, albeit with novel methods. Using her flair for show business, Phillips reinvented herself as the proprietor of Club Tsubaki, a high-end watering hole for Japanese officers and businessmen, where she drew out vital information from her patrons. Phillips's wartime experiences recounted in *Manila Espionage* are helpful in corroborating Japanese atrocities at Fort Santiago, where Phillips was briefly imprisoned and tortured, and the hardships imposed on the internees at Santo Tomas, who were already showing signs of expiring from starvation when the 1st Cavalry's flying columns rescued them. Unfortunately, a recent book by the American journalist Peter Eisner, *MacArthur's Spies* (2017), debunks substantial portions of Phillips's memoir. Although he does contend Phillips's own work as an asset for the guerrilla resistance was true, the circumstances of these exploits are rather seedy.

The burden of reconstructing the battle to liberate Manila forced other texts upon me. The challenge I faced in the months and weeks spent just mentally piecing together the four weeks of combat in February 1945 was assembling a narrative from so many different yarns. There was the urgency of XIV Corps to reach Manila, the 11th Airborne's own race to the city and the difficulties it faced against the Genko Line, the nearly impossible task of finding the motivations behind Rear Admiral Iwabuchi's death wish, the living hell for the civilians trapped in Manila's adjacent neighbourhoods still controlled by the Japanese, and finally the unanswered questions neglected by voluminous documentation from the war. To my disappointment, and this is a flaw I'll readily admit, American sources prevailed in the miniscule odyssey it took for learning everything that could be learned about the battle. Finding an equal variety of Japanese texts that revisited the subject was a fruitless effort.

A wonderful discovery was a small selection of war memoirs from the very commanders who fought across the South West Pacific's length and breadth. General Robert Eichelberger's *Our Jungle Road To Tokyo* ranks as a fine chronicle of the ground and air campaigns to roll back Japan's grip on Southeast Asia. His descriptions of the blitz across Luzon and the fighting that dragged on for months after Manila's liberation serve up useful insights on the combat that took place. A worthy companion to Eichelberger's account is the remarkable *The Angels: A History of the 11th Airborne Division* by Major Edward M. Flanagan Jr. Possessing the same scope as Eichelberger's memoir, as its title indicates *The Angels* follows all the major actions involving the unit and provides maps and ample photographs. It's a truly useful reference for learning about an elite infantry division's role in the Luzon campaign. Another fine complement to *Jungle Road* and *The Angels* is *General Kenney Reports: A Personal History of the Pacific War* by George C. Kenney that explains the role of air power in the same theatre where Eichelberger and many other talented generals served. A less ponderous read in the same setting that doesn't involve the battle of Manila is *Red Arrow Men: Stories About The 32nd Division On The Villa Verde* by John M. Carlisle. Rather than straight history, its more than 200 pages comprise short essays on the Luzon campaign that occasionally describes how Filipinos from all walks of life coped with wartime conditions.

In order to fortify my own knowledge about the battle, a different venue supplied additional material I needed. Thanks to the US government's vast online presence, the Defence Technical Information Center or DTIC (https://discover.dtic.mil) unearthed a trove of research—analytical treatises and master's theses—that brought the combat to vivid detail. The most accessible among the lot is 'The XIV Corps Battle for Manila February 1945' by Kevin T. McEnery that really provides so much context to the twists and turns that defined the confrontation between Iwabuchi's diehards and the Americans who crushed them. But the thesis isn't without its faults and I spotted some factual errors as I pored over its typewritten pages. A suitable companion to McEnery is the *Combat Studies Institute Battlebook 13-B: Battle of Manila* that reads like an after-action report for

XIV Corps. Another decent resource was *The Yamashita Decision* by Lieutenant Colonel William R. Branch that picks apart the war crimes trial of the general tasked with defending the Philippines at all costs. To learn the story behind Yamashita's downfall presents an interesting legalistic tangle. Since he never ordered any atrocities against Filipino and Western civilians, how was the highest-ranking Japanese commander supposed to be prosecuted of any crime? This isn't a straightforward case of 'command responsibility' since every account from the war shows what a fine mess Japanese military operations were by late 1944. But *The Yamashita Decision* was valuable to me as it furnished extra material on how awful the Japanese were toward Filipino civilians. This was a serious hurdle as I hammered out the most important chapters on the battle. As the Americans closed in, the Japanese Rikusentai holding Manila against the odds indiscriminately targeted civilians and killed untold numbers. I never hesitate to point out, in fact, the 100,000 innocent people who died in the battle is a rounded-off figure that is not corroborated by any database or index. While anecdotal and testimonial evidence of Japanese brutality are easy to find in newspaper archives and official statements during commemorative dates, rigorous documentation on these outrages are elusive. This compels me to confess another fault: financial limitations and time constraints prevented me from seeking out any survivors who lived through the battle. Hence, the best course of action was assembling as big a library of reading material on the battle that I could manage.

A true and wholly unexpected godsend, however, was the *Official Gazette* (officialgazette.gov.ph) that serves as a repository for the Philippine government's circulars, memoranda, and other public documents. Once again, the assiduous manipulation of the search bar brought out official remarks and transcripts dating from the post-war years. Of particular value were commemorations devoted to Filipino veterans and browsing through the stories brought the era they lived through to life. Next to the *Official Gazette*, the portal for Malacañang Palace (malacanang.gov.ph), which is the official residence for Filipino heads of state, has its own digitized archives on the post-war presidencies that furnished additional trivia. Unfortunately, I can't assign the same generous praise to local media here in the Philippines, whose columnists are guilty of neglecting the country's ordeal in World War II, and sifting through old newspaper clippings that have been digitized wasn't as rewarding as I thought. One ill-deserved meme that some writers have pushed recently is to blame American soldiers for the civilian death toll in Manila. While it is true the fighting was indiscriminate, Filipino revisionists who harbour anti-American sentiments ignore how Iwabuchi's Rikusentai chose an urban warfare doctrine that exploited civilian hostages and put them in harm's way. I'm certain the deployment of heavy artillery by American forces did result in some collateral damage, but other factors besides this caused the battle to be as dreadful as it turned out. Now as to why the Japanese defenders of Manila put so much energy in killing unarmed Filipinos, a definitive explanation for what motivated them remains elusive.

Finally, one particular resource that aided the descriptions on kit, weapons and technology is the one-man online endeavour World War II Database (ww2db.com) run by the enthusiast C. Peter Chen. When the convenient summaries on ww2db.com didn't

The World War II Manila American Cemetery and Memorial is located about six miles southeast of Manila, within the limits of Fort Bonifacio, the former U.S. Army Fort William McKinley. (American Battle Monuments Commission)

suffice, I checked the truly impressive *Handbook on Japanese Military Forces* published by the War Department in September 1944 to see what American analysts at the time had gleaned from Japanese equipment and weapons. The *Handbook*, by the way, is available as a free download on archive.org and is an irresistible must-have for anyone with a passion for World War II militaria. I do hope readers appreciate the final result of all this strenuous research. Fresh attempts at retelling the battle of Manila are published decades apart and there are precious few specialists in the subject. No wonder so many aspects of the battle seem baffling and impenetrable even for the most dedicated researcher struggling to assemble a riveting book against the odds. I can relate because I went through the same ordeal finishing my own book on the battle. May it serve readers well and stand the test of time.

Index